THE LEGENDS OF SAINT PATRICK

BY

AUBREY DE VERE, LL.D.

First published in 1872

Published by Left of Brain Books

Copyright © 2023 Left of Brain Books

ISBN 978-1-397-66646-8

First Edition

All rights reserved. No part of this publication may be reproduced, distributed, or transmitted in any form or by any means, including photocopying, recording, or other electronic or mechanical methods, without the prior written permission of the publisher, except in the case of brief quotations permitted by copyright law. Left of Brain Books is a division of Left Of Brain Onboarding Pty Ltd.

PUBLISHER'S PREFACE

About the Book

"Saint Patrick (Latin: Patricius, Irish: Naomh Padraig) was a Roman Britain-born Christian missionary and is the patron saint of Ireland along with Brigid of Kildare and Columba. When he was about sixteen he was captured by Irish raiders and taken as a slave to Ireland, where he lived for six years before escaping and returning to his family. He entered the church, as his father and grandfather had before him, becoming a deacon and a bishop. He later returned to Ireland as a missionary in the north and west of the island, but little is known about the places where he worked and no link can be made between Patrick and any church. By the eighth century he had become the patron saint of Ireland. The Irish monastery system evolved after the time of Patrick and the Irish church did not develop the diocesan model that Patrick and the other early missionaries had tried to establish."

(Quote from wikipedia.org)

About the Author

Aubrey Thomas de Vere (1814 - 1902)

"Aubrey Thomas de Vere (10 January 1814-20 January 1902) was an Irish poet and critic.

He was born at Curragh Chase, Kilcornan, County Limerick, the third son of Sir Aubrey de Vere Hunt (1788-1846) and younger brother to Stephen De Vere. In 1832 his father dropped the final name by royal licence. Sir Aubrey was himself a poet. Wordsworth called his sonnets the most perfect of the age. These and his drama, Mary Tudor, were published by his son in 1875 and 1884. Aubrey Thomas was educated at Trinity College, Dublin, and in his twenty-eighth year published The Waldenses, which he followed up in the next year by The Search after Proserpine. Thenceforward he was continually engaged, till his death in 1902, in the production of poetry and criticism.

His best-known works are: in verse, The Sisters (1861); The Infant Bridal (1864); Irish Odes (1869); Legends of St Patrick (1872); and Legends of the Saxon Saints (1879); and in prose, Essays chiefly on Poetry (1887); and Essays chiefly Literary and Ethical (1889). He also wrote a picturesque volume of travel-sketches, and two dramas in verse, Alexander the Great (1874); and St Thomas of Canterbury (1876); both of which, though they contain fine passages, suffer from diffuseness and a lack of dramatic spirit. His best remembered poem is Inisfail.

The characteristics of Aubrey de Vere's poetry are high seriousness and a fine religious enthusiasm. His research in questions of faith led him to the Roman Church; and in many of his poems, notably in the volume of sonnets called St Peters Chains (1888), he made rich additions to devotional verse. He was a disciple of Wordsworth, whose calm meditative serenity he often echoed with great felicity; and his affection for Greek poetry, truly felt and understood, gave dignity and weight to his own versions of mythological idylls. But perhaps he will be chiefly remembered for the impulse which he gave to the study of Celtic legend and Celtic literature. In this direction he has had many followers, who have sometimes assumed the appearance of pioneers; but after Matthew Arnold's fine lecture on Celtic Literature, nothing perhaps did more to help the Celtic revival than Aubrey de Vere's tender insight into the Irish character, and his stirring reproductions of the early Irish epic poetry."

(Quote from wikipedia.org)

CONTENTS

PUBLISHER'S PREFACE
INTRODUCTION BY HENRY MORLEY 1
SAINT PATRICK - FROM "ENGLISH WRITERS," BY HENRY MORLEY 3
AUTHOR'S PREFACE TO "THE LEGENDS OF SAINT PATRICK" 8
    THE BAPTISM OF ST. PATRICK.. 13
    THE DISBELIEF OF MILCHO, OR, SAINT PATRICK'S ONE FAILURE................. 14
    SAINT PATRICK AT TARA 30
    SAINT PATRICK AND THE TWO PRINCESSES 33
    SAINT PATRICK AND THE CHILDREN OF FOCHLUT WOOD............................ 39
    THE LAY OF THE HEADS... 46
    SAINT PATRICK AND KING LAEGHAIRE... 55
    SAINT PATRICK AND THE IMPOSTOR; OR, MAC KYLE OF MAN...................... 57
    SAINT PATRICK AT CASHEL; OR, THE BAPTISM OF AENGUS 63
    SAINT PATRICK AND THE CHILDLESS MOTHER 70
    SAINT PATRICK AT THE FEAST OF KNOCK CAE; OR, THE FOUNDING OF
    MUNGRET 77
    SAINT PATRICK AND KING EOCHAID 87
    SAINT PATRICK AND THE FOUNDING OF ARMAGH CATHEDRAL 100
    THE ARRAIGNMENT OF SAINT PATRICK... 112
    THE STRIVING OF SAINT PATRICK ON MOUNT CRUACHAN......................... 123
    EPILOGUE. THE CONFESSION OF SAINT PATRICK 137

INTRODUCTION BY HENRY MORLEY

ONCE more our readers are indebted to a living poet for wide circulation of a volume of delightful verse. The name of Aubrey de Vere is the more pleasantly familiar because its association with our highest literature has descended from father to son. In 1822, sixty-seven years ago, Sir Aubrey de Vere, of Curragh Chase, by Adare, in the county of Limerick - then thirty-four years old - first made his mark with a dramatic poem upon "Julian the Apostate." In 1842 Sir Aubrey published Sonnets, which his friend Wordsworth described as "the most perfect of our age;" and in the year of his death he completed a dramatic poem upon "Mary Tudor," published in the next year, 1847, with the "Lamentation of Ireland, and other Poems." Sir Aubrey de Vere's "Mary Tudor" should be read by all who have read Tennyson's play on the same subject.

The gift of genius passed from Sir Aubrey to his third son, Aubrey Thomas de Vere, who was born in 1814, and through a long life has put into music only noble thoughts associated with the love of God and man, and of his native land. His first work, published forty-seven years ago, was a lyrical piece, in which he gave his sympathy to devout and persecuted men whose ways of thought were not his own. Aubrey de Vere's poems have been from time to time revised by himself, and they were in 1884 finally collected into three volumes, published by Messrs. Kegan Paul. Left free to choose from among their various contents, I have taken this little book of "Legends of St. Patrick," first published in 1872, but in so doing I have unwillingly left many a piece that would please many a reader.

They are not, however, inaccessible. Of the three volumes of collected works, each may be had separately, and is complete in itself. The first contains "The Search after Proserpine, and other Poems - Classical and Meditative." The second contains the "Legends of St. Patrick, and Legends of Ireland's Heroic Age," including a version of the "Tain Bo." The third contains two plays, "Alexander the Great," "St. Thomas of Canterbury," and other Poems.

For the convenience of some readers, the following extract from the second volume of my "English Writers," may serve as a prosaic summary of what is actually known about St. Patrick.

H. M.

SAINT PATRICK - FROM "ENGLISH WRITERS," BY HENRY MORLEY

THE birth of St. Patrick, Apostle and Saint of Ireland, has been generally placed in the latter half of the fourth century; and he is said to have died at the age of a hundred and twenty. As he died in the year 493 - and we may admit that he was then a very old man - if we may say that he reached the age of eighty-eight, we place his birth in the year 405. We may reasonably believe, therefore, that he was born in the early part of the fifth century. His birthplace, now known as Kilpatrick, was at the junction of the Levin with the Clyde, in what is now the county of Dumbarton. His baptismal name was Succath. His father was Calphurnius, a deacon, son of Potitus, who was a priest. His mother's name was Conches-sa, whose family may have belonged to Gaul, and who may thus have been, as it is said she was, of the kindred of St. Martin of Tours; for there is a tradition that she was with Calphurnius as a slave before he married her. Since Eusebius spoke of three bishops from Britain at the Council of Arles, Succath, known afterwards in missionary life by his name in religion, Patricius (pater civium), might very reasonably be a deacon's son.

In his early years Succath was at home by the Clyde, and he speaks of himself as not having been obedient to the teaching of the clergy. When he was sixteen years old he, with two of his sisters and other of his countrymen, was seized by a band of Irish pirates that made descent on the shore of the Clyde and carried him off to slavery. His sisters were taken to another part of the island, and he was sold to Milcho MacCuboin in the north, whom he served for six or seven years, so learning to speak the language of the country, while keeping his master's sheep by the Mountain of Slieve Miss. Thoughts of home and of its Christian life made the youth feel the heathenism that was about him; his exile seemed to him a punishment for boyish indifference; and during the years when young enthusiasm looks out upon life with new sense of a man's power - growing for man's work that is to do - Succath became filled with religious zeal.

Three Latin pieces are ascribed to St. Patrick: a "Confession," which is in the Book of Armagh, and in three other manuscripts; [1] a letter to Coroticus, and a few "Dieta Patricii," which are also in the Book of Armagh. [2] There is no strong reason for questioning the authenticity of the "Confession," which is in unpolished Latin, the writer calling himself "indoctus, rusticissimus, imperitus," and it is full of a deep religious feeling. It is concerned rather with the inner than the outer life, but includes references to the early days of trial by which Succath's whole heart was turned to God. He says, "After I came into Ireland I pastured sheep daily, and prayed many times a day. The love and fear of God, and faith and spirit, wrought in me more and more, so that in one day I reached to a hundred prayers, and in the night almost as many, and stayed in the woods and on the mountains, and was urged to prayer before the dawn, in snow, in frost, in rain, and took no harm, nor, I think, was there any sloth in me. And there one night I heard a voice in a dream saying to me, 'Thou hast well fasted; thou shalt go back soon to thine own land;' and again after a little while, 'Behold! thy ship is ready.'" In all this there is the passionate longing of an ardent mind for home and Heaven.

At the age of twenty-two Succath fled from his slavery to a vessel of which the master first refused and finally consented to take him on board. He and the sailors were then cast by a storm upon a desert shore of Britain, possibly upon some region laid waste by ravages from over sea. Having at last made his way back, by a sea passage, to his home on the Clyde, Succath was after a time captured again, but remained captive only for two months, and went back home. Then the zeal for his Master's service made him feel like the Seafarer in the Anglo-Saxon poem; and all the traditions of his home would have accorded with the rise of the resolve to cross the sea, and to spread Christ's teaching in what had been the land of his captivity.

There were already centres of Christian work in Ireland, where devoted men were labouring and drew a few into their fellowship. Succath aimed at the gathering of all these scattered forces, by a movement that should

---

[1] Cotton MSS., Nero, E.'; Codex Salisburiensis; and a MS. in the Monastery of St. Vaast.

[2] The Book of Armagh, preserved at Trinity College, Dublin, contains a Life of St. Patrick, with his writings, and consists in chief part of a description of all the books of the New Testament, including the Epistle of Paul to the Laodiceans. Traces found here and there of the name of the copyist and of the archbishop for whom the copy was made, fix its date almost to a year as 807 or 811-812.

carry with it the whole people. He first prepared himself by giving about four years to study of the Scriptures at Auxerre, under Germanus, and then went to Rome, under the conduct of a priest, Segetius, and probably with letters from Germanus to Pope Celestine. Whether he received his orders from the Pope seems doubtful; but the evidence is strong that Celestine sent him on his Irish mission. Succath left Rome, passed through North Italy and Gaul, till he met on his way two followers of Palladius, Augustinus and Benedictus, who told him of their master's failure, and of his death at Fordun. Succath then obtained consecration from Amathus, a neighbouring bishop, and as Patricius, went straight to Ireland. He landed near the town of Wicklow, by the estuary of the River Varty, which had been the landing-place of Palladius. In that region he was, like Palladius, opposed; but he made some conversions, and advanced with his work northward that he might reach the home of his old master, Milcho, and pay him the purchase-money of his stolen freedom. But Milcho, it is said, burnt himself and his goods rather than bear the shame of submission to the growing power of his former slave.

St. Patrick addressed the ruling classes, who could bring with them their followers, and he joined tact with his zeal; respecting ancient prejudices, opposing nothing that was not directly hostile to the spirit of Christianity, and handling skilfully the chiefs with whom he had to deal. An early convert - Dichu MacTrighim - was a chief with influential connections, who gave the ground for the religious house now known as Saul. This chief satisfied so well the inquiries of Laeghaire, son of Niall, King of Erin, concerning the stranger's movements, that St. Patrick took ship for the mouth of the Boyne, and made his way straight to the king himself. The result of his energy was that he met successfully all the opposition of those who were concerned in the maintenance of old heathen worship, and brought King Laeghaire to his side.

Then Laeghaire resolved that the old laws of the country as established by the judges, whose order was named Brehon, should be revised, and brought into accord with the new teaching. So the Brehon laws of Ireland were revised, with St. Patrick's assistance, and there were no ancient customs broken or altered, except those that could not be harmonised with Christian teaching. The good sense of St. Patrick enabled this great work to be done without offence to the people. The collection of laws thus made by the chief lawyers of the time, with the assistance of St. Patrick, is known as the "Senchus Mor," and, says an old poem -

> "Laeghaire, Corc Dairi, the brave;
> Patrick, Beuen, Cairnech, the just;
> Rossa, Dubtach, Fergus, the wise;
> These are the nine pillars of the Senchus Mor."

This body of laws, traditions, and treatises on law is found in no manuscript of a date earlier than the fourteenth century. It includes, therefore, much that is of later date than the fifth century.

St. Patrick's greatest energies are said to have been put forth in Ulster and Leinster. Among the churches or religious communities founded by him in Ulster was that of Armagh. If he was born about the year 405, when he was carried to Ireland as a prisoner at the age of sixteen the date would have been 421. His age would have been twenty-two when he escaped, after six or seven years of captivity, and the date 427. A year at home, and four years with Germanus at Auxerre, would bring him to the age of twenty-seven, and the year 432, when he began his great endeavour to put Christianity into the main body of the Irish people. That work filled all the rest of his life, which was long. If we accept the statement, in which all the old records agree, that the time of Patrick's labour in Ireland was not less than sixty years; sixty years bring him to the age of eighty-eight in the year 493. And in that year he died.

The "Letter to Coroticus," ascribed to St. Patrick, is addressed to a petty king of Brittany who persecuted Christians, and was meant for the encouragement of Christian soldiers who served under him. It may, probably, be regarded as authentic. The mass of legend woven into the life of the great missionary lies outside this piece and the "Confession." The "Confession" only expresses heights and depths of religious feeling haunted by impressions and dreams, through which, to the fervid nature out of which they sprang heaven seemed to speak. St. Patrick did not attack heresies among the Christians; he preached to those who were not Christians the Christian faith and practice. His great influence was not that of a writer, but of a speaker. He must have been an orator, profoundly earnest, who could put his soul into his voice; and, when his words bred deeds, conquered all difficulties in the way of action with right feeling and good sense.

HENRY MORLEY.

TO THE MEMORY OF WORDSWORTH.

AUTHOR'S PREFACE TO "THE LEGENDS OF SAINT PATRICK"

THE ancient records of Ireland abound in legends respecting the greatest man and the greatest benefactor that ever trod her soil; and of these the earlier are at once the more authentic and the nobler. Not a few have a character of the sublime; many are pathetic; some have a profound meaning under a strange disguise; but their predominant character is their brightness and gladsomeness. A large tract of Irish history is dark: but the time of Saint Patrick, and the three centuries which succeeded it, were her time of joy. That chronicle is a song of gratitude and hope, as befits the story of a nation's conversion to Christianity, and in it the bird and the brook blend their carols with those of angels and of men. It was otherwise with the later legends connecting Ossian with Saint Patrick. A poet once remarked, while studying the frescoes of Michael Angelo in the Sistine Chapel, that the Sibyls are always sad, while the Prophets alternated with them are joyous. In the legends of the Patrician Cycle the chief-loving old Bard is ever mournful, for his face is turned to the past glories of his country; while the Saint is always bright, because his eyes are set on to the glory that has no end.

These legends are to be found chiefly in several very ancient lives of Saint Patrick, the most valuable of which is the "Tripartite Life," ascribed by Colgan to the century after the Saint's death, though it has not escaped later interpolations. The work was long lost, but two copies of it were rediscovered, one of which has been recently translated by that eminent Irish scholar, Mr. Hennessy. Whether regarded from the religious or the philosophic point of view, few things can be more instructive than the picture which it delineates of human nature at a period of critical transition, and the dawning of the Religion of Peace upon a race barbaric, but far indeed from savage. That wild race regarded it doubtless as a notable cruelty when the new Faith discouraged an amusement so popular as battle; but in many respects they were in sympathy with that Faith. It was one in which the nobler affections, as well as the passions, retained an unblunted ardour; and where Nature is strongest and least corrupted it most feels the need of something higher than itself, its interpreter and its supplement. It prized the family ties, like the Germans recorded by Tacitus; and it could not but have been drawn to Christianity, which consecrated them. Its morals were pure, and it had not lost that simplicity to which so much of spiritual insight belongs. Admiration and wonder were among its chief habits; and it would not have been repelled by Mysteries in what professed to belong to the Infinite. Lawless as it was, it abounded also in loyalty, generosity, and self-sacrifice; it was not, therefore, untouched by the records of martyrs, examples of self-sacrifice, or the doctrine of a great Sacrifice. It loved children and the poor; and Christianity made the former the exemplars of faith, and the latter the eminent inheritors of the Kingdom. On the other hand, all the vices of the race ranged themselves against the new religion.

In the main the institutions and traditions of Ireland were favourable to Christianity. She had preserved in a large measure the patriarchal system of the East. Her clans were families, and her chiefs were patriarchs who led their households to battle, and seized or recovered the spoil. To such a people the Christian Church announced herself as a great family - the family of man. Her genealogies went up to the first parent, and her rule was parental rule. The kingdom of Christ was the household of Christ; and its children in all lands formed the tribes of a larger Israel. Its laws were living traditions; and for traditions the Irish had ever retained the Eastern reverence.

In the Druids no formidable enemy was found; it was the Bards who wielded the predominant social influence. As in Greece, where the sacerdotal power was small, the Bards were the priests of the national Imagination, and round them all moral influences had gathered themselves. They were jealous of their rivals; but those rivals won them by degrees. Secknall and Fiacc were Christian Bards, trained by St. Patrick, who is said to have also brought a bard with him from Italy. The beautiful legend in which the Saint loosened the tongue of the dumb child was an apt emblem of Christianity imparting to the Irish race the highest use of its natural faculties. The Christian clergy turned to account the Irish traditions, as they had made use of the Pagan temples, purifying them first. The Christian religion looked with a genuine kindness on whatever was human, except so far as the stain was on it; and while it resisted to the face what was unchristian in spirit, it also, in the Apostolic sense, "made itself all things to all men." As legislator, Saint Patrick waged no needless war against the ancient laws of Ireland. He purified them, and he amplified them, discarding only what was unfit for a nation made Christian. Thus was produced the great "Book of the Law," or "Senchus Mohr," compiled A.D. 439.

The Irish received the Gospel gladly. The great and the learned, in other nations the last to believe, among them commonly set the example. With the natural disposition of the race an appropriate culture had concurred. It was one which at least did not fail to develop the imagination, the affections, and a great part of the moral being, and which thus indirectly prepared ardent natures, and not less the heroic than the tender, to seek their rest in spiritual things, rather than in material or conventional. That culture, without removing the barbaric, had blended it with the refined. It had created among the people an appreciation of the beautiful, the pathetic, and the pure. The early Irish chronicles, as well as songs, show how strong among them that sentiment had ever been. The Borromean Tribute, for so many ages the source of relentless wars, had been imposed in vengeance for an insult offered to a woman; and a discourtesy shown to a poet had overthrown an ancient dynasty. The education of an Ollambh occupied twelve years; and in the third century, the time of Oiseen and Fionn, the military rules of the Feinè included provisions which the chivalry of later ages might have been proud of. It was a wild, but not wholly an ungentle time. An unprovoked affront was regarded as a grave moral offence; and severe punishments were ordained, not only for detraction, but for a word, though uttered in jest, which brought a blush on the cheek of a listener. Yet an injury a hundred years old could meet no forgiveness, and the life of man was war! It was not that laws were wanting; a code, minute in its justice, had proportioned a penalty to every offence, and specified the *Eric* which was to wipe out the bloodstain in case the injured party renounced his claim to right his own wrong. It was not that hearts were hard - there was at least as much pity for others as for self. It was that anger was implacable, and that where fear was unknown, the war field was what among us the hunting field is.

The rapid growth of learning as well as piety in the three centuries succeeding the conversion of Ireland, prove that the country had not been till then without a preparation for the gift. It had been the special skill of Saint Patrick to build the good which was lacked upon that which existed. Even the material arts of Ireland he had pressed into the service of the Faith; and Irish craftsmen had assisted him, not only in the building of his churches, but in casting his church bells, and in the adornment of his chalices, crosiers, and ecclesiastical vestments. Once elevated by Christianity, Ireland's early civilisation was a memorable thing. It sheltered a high virtue at home, and evangelised a great part of Northern Europe; and amidst many confusions it held its own till the true time of barbarism had set in - those two disastrous centuries when the Danish invasions trod down the sanctuaries, dispersed the libraries, and laid waste the colleges to which distant kings had sent their sons.

Perhaps nothing human had so large an influence in the conversion of the Irish as the personal character of her Apostle. Where others, as Palladius, had failed, he succeeded. By nature, by grace, and by providential training, he had been specially fitted for his task. We can still see plainly even the finer traits of that character, while the land of his birth is a matter of dispute, and of his early history we know little, except that he was of noble birth, that he was carried to Ireland by pirates at the age of sixteen, and that after five years of bondage he escaped thence, to return A.D. 432, when about forty-five years old; belonging thus to that great age of the Church which was made illustrious by the most eminent of its Fathers, and tasked by the most critical of its trials. In him a great character had been built on the foundations of a devout childhood, and of a youth ennobled by adversity. Everywhere we trace the might and the sweetness which belonged to it, the versatile mind yet the simple heart, the varying tact yet the fixed resolve, the large design taking counsel for all, yet the minute solicitude for each, the fiery zeal yet the genial temper, the skill in using means yet the reliance on God alone, the readiness in action with the willingness to wait, the habitual self-possession yet the outbursts of an inspiration which raised him above himself, the abiding consciousness of authority - an authority in him, but not of him - and yet the ever-present humility. Above all, there burned in him that boundless love, which seems the main constituent of the Apostolic character. It was love for God; but it was love for man also, an impassioned love, and a parental compassion. It was not for the spiritual weal alone of man that he thirsted. Wrong and injustice to the poor he resented as an injury to God. His vehement love for the poor is illustrated by his "Epistle to Coroticus," reproaching him with his cruelty, as well as by his denunciations of slavery, which piracy had introduced into parts of Ireland. No wonder that such a character should have exercised a talismanic power over the ardent and sensitive race among whom he laboured, a race "easy to be drawn, but impossible to be driven," and drawn more by sympathy than even by benefits. That character can only be understood by one who studies, and in a right spirit, that account of his life which he bequeathed to us shortly before its close - the "Confession of Saint Patrick." The last poem in this series embodies its most characteristic portions, including the visions which it records.

The "Tripartite Life" thus ends: - "After these great miracles, therefore, after resuscitating the dead, after healing lepers, and the blind, and the deaf, and the lame, and all diseases; after ordaining bishops, and priests, and deacons, and people of all orders in the Church; after teaching the men of Erin, and after baptising them; after founding churches and monasteries; after destroying idols and images and Druidical arts, the hour of death of Saint Patrick approached. He received the body of Christ from the Bishop Tassach, according to the counsel of the Angel Victor. He resigned his spirit afterwards to Heaven, in the one hundred and twentieth year of his age. His body is still here in the earth, with honour and reverence. Though great his honour here, greater honour will be to him in the Day of Judgment, when judgment will be given on the fruit of his teaching, as of every great Apostle, in the union of the Apostles and Disciples of Jesus; in the union of the Nine Orders of Angels, which cannot be surpassed; in the union of the Divinity and Humanity of the Son of God; in the union, which is higher than all unions, of the Holy Trinity, Father, Son, and Holy Ghost."

A. DE VERE.

THE LEGENDS OF SAINT PATRICK.

THE BAPTISM OF ST. PATRICK

"How can the babe baptiséd be
Where font is none and water none?"
Thus wept the nurse on bended knee,
And swayed the Infant in the sun.

"The blind priest took that Infant's hand:
With that small hand, above the ground
He signed the Cross. At God's command
A fountain rose with brimming bound.

"In that pure wave from Adam's sin
The blind priest cleansed the Babe with awe;
Then, reverently, he washed therein
His old, unseeing face, and saw!

"He saw the earth; he saw the skies,
And that all-wondrous Child decreed
A pagan nation to baptise,
To give the Gentiles light indeed."

Thus Secknall sang. Far off and nigh
The clansmen shouted loud and long;
While every mother tossed more high
Her babe, and glorying joined the song.

THE DISBELIEF OF MILCHO, OR, SAINT PATRICK'S ONE FAILURE

Fame of St. Patrick goes ever before him, and men of goodwill believe gladly; but Milcho, a mighty merchant, and one given wholly to pride and greed, wills to disbelieve. St. Patrick sends him greeting and gifts; but he, discovering that the prophet welcomed by all had once been his slave, hates him the more. Notwithstanding, he fears that when that prophet arrives, he, too, may be forced to believe, though against his will. He resolves to set fire to his castle and all his wealth, and make new fortunes in far lands. The doom of Milcho, who willed to disbelieve.

When now at Imber Dea that precious bark
Freighted with Erin's future, touched the sands
Just where a river, through a woody vale
Curving, with duskier current clave the sea,
Patrick, the Island's great inheritor,
His perilous voyage past, stept forth and knelt
And blessed his God. The peace of those green meads
Cradled 'twixt purple hills and purple deep,
Seemed as the peace of heaven. The sun had set;
But still those summits twinned, the "Golden Spears,"
Laughed with his latest beam. The hours went by:
The brethren paced the shore or musing sat,
But still their Patriarch knelt and still gave thanks
For all the marvellous chances of his life
Since those his earlier years when, slave new-trapped,
He comforted on hills of Dalaraide
His hungry heart with God, and, cleansed by pain,
In exile found the spirit's native land.
Eve deepened into night, and still he prayed:
The clear cold stars had crowned the azure vault;
And, risen at midnight from dark seas, the moon
Had quenched those stars, yet Patrick still prayed on:
Till from the river murmuring in the vale,
Far off, and from the morning airs close by

That shook the alders by the river's mouth,
And from his own deep heart a voice there came,
"Ere yet thou fling'st God's bounty on this land
There is a debt to cancel. Where is he,
Thy five years' lord that scourged thee for his swine?
Alas that wintry face! Alas that heart
Joyless since earliest youth! To him reveal it!
To him declare that God who Man became
To raise man's fall'n estate, as though a man,
All faculties of man unmerged, undimmed,
Had changed to worm and died the prey of worms,
That so the mole might see!"

Thus Patrick mused
Not ignorant that from low beginnings rise
Oftenest the works of greatness; yet of this
Unweeting, that his failure, one and sole
Through all his more than mortal course, even now
Before that low beginning's threshold lay,
Betwixt it and that Promised Land beyond
A bar of scandal stretched. Not otherwise
Might whatsoe'er was mortal in his strength
Dying, put on the immortal.

With the morn
Deep sleep descended on him. Waking soon,
He rose a man of might, and in that might
Laboured; and God His servant's toil revered;
And gladly on that coast Erin to Christ
Paid her firstfruits. Three days he preached his Lord:
The fourth embarking, cape succeeding cape
They passed, and heard the lowing herds remote
In hollow glens, and smelt the balmy breath
Of gorse on golden hillsides; till at eve,
The Imber Domnand reached, on silver sands
Grated their keel. Around them flocked at dawn
Warriors with hunters mixed, and shepherd youths
And maids with lips as red as mountain berries
And eyes like sloes, or keener eyes, dark-fringed
And gleaming like the blue-black spear. They came

With milk-pail, and with kid, and kindled fire
And spread the genial board. Upon that shore
Full many knelt and gave themselves to Christ,
Strong men, and men at midmost of their hopes
By sickness felled; old chiefs, at life's dim close
That oft had asked, "Beyond the grave what hope?"
Worn sailors weary of the toilsome seas,
And craving rest; they, too, that sex which wears
The blended crowns of Chastity and Love;
Wondering, they hailed the Maiden-Motherhood;
And listening children praised the Babe Divine,
And passed Him, each to each.

Ere long, once more
Their sails were spread. Again by grassy marge
They rowed, and sylvan glades. The branching deer
Like flying gleams went by them. Oft the cry
Of fighting clans rang out: but oftener yet
Clamour of rural dance, or mart confused
With many-coloured garb and movements swift,
Pageant sun-bright: or on the sands a throng
Girdled with circle glad some bard whose song
Shook the wild clan as tempest shakes the woods.
Still north the wanderers sailed: at evening, mists
Cumbered the shore and on them leaned the blast,
And fierce rain flashed mingling with dim-lit sea.
All night they toiled; next day at noon they kenned
A seaward stream that shone like golden tress
Severed and random-thrown. That river's mouth
Ere long attained was all with lilies white
As April field with daisies. Entering there
They reached a wood, and disembarked with joy:
There, after thanks to God, silent they sat
In thought, and watched the ripples, dusk yet bright,
That lived and died like things that laughed at time,
On gliding 'neath those many-centuried boughs.
But, midmost, Patrick slept. Then through the trees,
Shy as a fawn half-tamed now stole, now fled
A boy of such bright aspect faëry child
He seemed, or babe exposed of royal race:

At last assured beside the Saint he stood,
And dropped on him a flower, and disappeared:
Thus flower on flower from the great wood he brought
And hid them in the bosom of the Saint.
The monks forbade him, saying, "Lest thou wake
The master from his sleep." But Patrick woke,
And saw the boy, and said, "Forbid him not;
The heir of all my kingdom is this child."
Then spake the brethren, "Wilt thou walk with us?"
And he, "I will:" and so for his sweet face
They called his name Benignus: and the boy
Thenceforth was Christ's. Beneath his parent's roof
At night they housed. Nowhere that child would sleep
Except at Patrick's feet. Till Patrick's death
Unchanged to him he clave, and after reigned
The second at Ardmacha.

Day by day
They held their course; ere long the hills of Mourne
Loomed through sea-mist: Ulidian summits next
Before them rose: but nearer at their left
Inland with westward channel wound the wave
Changed to sea-lake. Nine miles with chant and hymn
They tracked the gold path of the sinking sun;
Then southward ran 'twixt headland and green isle
And landed. Dewy pastures sunset-dazed,
At leisure paced by mild-eyed milk-white kine
Smiled them a welcome. Onward moved in sight
Swiftly, with shadow far before him cast,
Dichu, that region's lord, a martial man
And merry, and a speaker of the truth.
Pirates he deemed them first and toward them faced
With wolf-hounds twain that watched their master's eye
To spring, or not to spring. The imperious face
Forbidding not, they sprang; but Patrick raised
His hand, and stone-like crouched they chained and still:
Then, Dichu onward striding fierce, the Saint
Between them signed the Cross; and lo, the sword
Froze in his hand, and Dichu stood like stone.
The amazement past, he prayed the man of God

To grace his house; and, side by side, a mile
They clomb the hills. Ascending, Patrick turned,
His heart with prescience filled. Beneath, there lay
A gleaming strait; beyond, a dim vast plain
With many an inlet pierced: a golden marge
Girdled the water-tongues with flag and reed;
But, farther off, a gentle sea-mist changed
The fair green flats to purple. "Night comes on;"
Thus Dichu spake, and waited. Patrick then
Advanced once more, and Sabhall soon was reached,
A castle half, half barn. There garnered lay
Much grain, and sun-imbrowned: and Patrick said,
"Here where the earthly grain was stored for man
The bread of angels man shall eat one day."
And Patrick loved that place, and Patrick said,
"King Dichu, give thou to the poor that grain,
To Christ, our Lord, thy barn." The strong man stood
In doubt; but prayers of little orphaned babes
Reared by his hand, went up for him that hour:
Therefore that barn he ceded, and to Christ
By Patrick was baptised. Where lay the corn
A convent later rose. There dwelt he oft;
And 'neath its roof more late the stranger sat,
Exile, or kingdom-wearied king, or bard,
That haply blind in age, yet tempest-rocked
By memories of departed glories, drew
With gradual influx into his old heart
Solace of Christian hope.

With Dichu bode
Patrick somewhile, intent from him to learn
The inmost of that people. Oft they spake
Of Milcho. "Once his thrall, against my will
In earthly things I served him: for his soul
Needs therefore must I labour. Hard was he;
Unlike those hearts to which God's Truth makes way
Like message from a mother in her grave:
Yet what I can I must. Not heaven itself
Can force belief; for Faith is still good will."
Dichu laughed aloud: "Good will! Milcho's good will

Neither to others, nor himself, good will
Hath Milcho! Fireless sits he, winter through,
The logs beside his hearth: and as on them
Glimmers the rime, so glimmers on his face
The smile. Convert him! Better thrice to hang him!
Baptise him! He will film your font with ice!
The cold of Milcho's heart has winter-nipt
That glen he dwells in! From the sea it slopes
Unfinished, savage, like some nightmare dream,
Raked by an endless east wind of its own.
On wolf's milk was he suckled not on woman's!
To Milcho speed! Of Milcho claim belief!
Milcho will shrivel his small eye and say
He scorns to trust himself his father's son,
Nor deems his lands his own by right of race
But clutched by stress of brain! Old Milcho's God
Is gold. Forbear him, sir, or ere you seek him
Make smooth your way with gold."

Thus Dichu spake;
And Patrick, after musings long, replied:
"Faith is no gift that gold begets or feeds,
Oftener by gold extinguished. Unto God,
Unbribed, unpurchased, yearns the soul of man;
Yet finds perforce in God its great reward.
Not less this Milcho deems I did him wrong,
His slave, yet fleeing. To requite that loss
Gifts will I send him first by messengers
Ere yet I see his face."

Then Patrick sent
His messengers to Milcho, speaking thus:
"If ill befell thy herds through flight of mine
Fourfold that loss requite I, lest, for hate
Of me, thou disesteem my Master's Word.
Likewise I sue thy friendship; and I come
In few days' space, with gift of other gold
Than earth concedes, the Tidings of that God
Who made all worlds, and late His Face hath shown,
Sun-like to man. But thou, rejoice in hope!"

Thus Patrick, once by man advised in part,
Though wont to counsel with his God alone.

Meantime full many a rumour vague had vexed
Milcho much musing. He had dealings large
And distant. Died a chief? He sent and bought
The widow's all; or sold on foodless shores
For usury the leanest of his kine.
Meantime, his dark ships and the populous quays
With news still murmured. First from Imber Dea
Came whispers how a sage had landed late,
And how when Nathi fain had barred his way,
Nathi that spurned Palladius from the land,
That sage with levelled eyes, and kingly front
Had from his presence driven him with a ban
Cur-like and craven; how on bended knee
Sinell believed, the royal man well-loved
Descending from the judgment-seat with joy:
And how when fishers spurned his brethren's quest
For needful food, that sage had raised his rod,
And all the silver harvest of blue streams
Lay black in nets and sand. His wrinkled brow
Wrinkling yet more, thus Milcho answer made:
"Deceived are those that will to be deceived:
This knave has heard of gold in river-beds,
And comes a deft sand-groper; let him come!
He'll toil ten years ere gold enough he finds
To make a crooked torque."

From Tara next
The news: "Laeghaire, the King, sits close in cloud
Of sullen thought, or storms from court to court,
Because the chiefest of the Druid race
Locru, and Luchat prophesied long since
That one day from the sea a Priest would come
With Doctrine and a Rite, and dash to earth
Idols, and hurl great monarchs from their thrones;
And lo! At Imber Boindi late there stept
A priest from roaring waves with Creed and Rite,

And men before him bow." Then Milcho spake:
"Not flesh enough from thy strong bones, Laeghaire,
These Druids, ravens of the woods, have plucked,
But they must pluck thine eyes! Ah priestly race,
I loathe ye! 'Twixt the people and their King
Ever ye rub a sore!" Last came a voice:
"This day in Eire thy saying is fulfilled,
Conn of the 'Hundred Battles,' from thy throne
Leaping long since, and crying, 'O'er the sea
The Prophet cometh, princes in his train,
Bearing for regal sceptres bended staffs,
Which from the land's high places, cliff and peak,
Shall drag the fair flowers down!'" Scoffing he heard:
"Conn of the 'Hundred Battles!' Had he sent
His hundred thousand kernes to yonder steep
And rolled its boulders down, and built a mole
To fence my laden ships from spring-tide surge,
Far kinglier pattern had he shown, and given
More solace to the land."

He rose and turned
With sideway leer; and printing with vague step
Irregular the shining sands, on strode
Toward his cold home, alone; and saw by chance
A little bird light-perched, that, being sick,
Plucked from the fissured sea-cliff grains of sand;
And, noting, said, "O bird, when beak of thine
From base to crown hath gorged this huge sea-wall,
Then shall that man of Creed and Rite make null
The strong rock of my will!" Thus Milcho spake,
Feigning the peace not his.

Next day it chanced
Women he heard in converse. Thus the first:
"If true the news, good speed for him, my boy!
Poor slaves by Milcho scourged on earth shall wear
In heaven a monarch's crown! Good speed for her
His little sister, not reserved like us
To bend beneath these loads." To whom her mate:
"Doubt not the Prophet's tidings! Not in vain

The Power Unknown hath shaped us! Come He must,
Or send, and help His people on their way.
Good is He, or He ne'er had made these babes!"
They passed, and Milcho said, "Through hate of me
All men believe!" And straightway Milcho's face
Grew bleaker than that crab-tree stem forlorn
That hid him, wanner than that sea-sand wet
That whitened round his foot down-pressed.

Time passed.
One morn in bitter mockery Milcho mused:
"What better laughter than when thief from thief
Pilfers the pilfered goods? Our Druid thief
Two thousand years hath milked and shorn this land;
Now comes the thief outlandish that with him
Would share milk-pail and fleece! O Bacrach old,
To hear thee shout 'Impostor!'" Straight he went
To Bacrach's cell hid in a skirt wind-shav'n
Of low-grown wood, and met, departing thence,
Three sailors sea-tanned from a ship late-beached.
Within a corner huddled, on the floor,
The Druid sat, cowering, and cold, and mazed:
Sudden he rose, and cried, by conquering joy
Clothed as with youth restored: "The God Unknown,
That God who made the earth, hath walked the earth!
This hour His Prophet treads the isle! Three men
Have seen him; and their speech is true. To them
That Prophet spake: 'Four hundred years ago,
Sinless God's Son on earth for sinners died:
Black grew the world, and graves gave up their dead.'
Thus spake the Seer. Four hundred years ago!
Mark well the time! Of Ulster's Druid race
What man but yearly, those four hundred years,
Trembled that tale recounting which with this
Tallies as footprint with the foot of man?
Four hundred years ago - that self-same day -
Connor, the son of Nessa, Ulster's King,
Sat throned, and judged his people. As he sat,
Under clear skies, behold, o'er all the earth
Swept a great shadow from the windless east;

And darkness hung upon the air three hours;
Dead fell the birds, and beasts astonied fled.
Then to his Chief of Druids, Connor spake
Whispering; and he, his oracles explored,
Shivering made answer, 'From a land accursed,
O King, that shadow sweeps; therein, this hour,
By sinful men sinless God's Son is slain.'
Then Ulster's king, down-dashing sceptre and crown,
Rose, clamouring, 'Sinless! shall the sinless die?'
And madness fell on him; and down that steep
He rushed whereon the Emanian Palace stood,
And reached the grove, Lambraidhè, with two swords,
The sword of battle, and the sword of state,
And hewed and hewed, crying, 'Were I but there
Thus they should fall who slay that Sinless One;'
And in that madness died. Old Erin's sons
Beheld this thing; nor ever in the land
Hath ceased the rumour, nor the tear for him
Who, wroth at justice trampled, martyr died.
And now we know that not for any dream
He died, but for the truth: and whensoe'er
The Prophet of that Son of God who died
Sinless for sinners, standeth in this place,
I, Bacrach, oldest Druid in this Isle,
Will rise the first, and kiss his vesture's hem."

He spake; and Milcho heard, and without speech
Departed from that house.

A later day
When the wild March sunset, gone almost ere come,
By glacial shower was hustled out of life,
Under a blighted ash tree, near his house,
Thus mused the man: "Believe, or Disbelieve!
The will does both; Then idiot who would be
For profitless belief to sell himself?
Yet disbelief not less might work our bane!
For, I remember, once a sickly slave
Ill shepherded my flock: I spake him plain;
'When next, through fault of thine, the midnight wolf

Worries my sheep, on yonder tree you hang:'
The blear-eyed idiot looked into my face,
And smiled his disbelief. On that day week
Two lambs lay dead. I hanged him on a tree.
What tree? this tree! Why, this is passing strange!
For, three nights since, I saw him in a dream:
Weakling as wont he stood beside my bed,
And, clutching at his wrenched and livid throat,
Spake thus, 'Belief is safest.'"

Ceased the hail
To rattle on the ever barren boughs,
And friendlier sound was heard. Beside his door
Wayworn the messengers of Patrick stood,
And showed the gifts, and held his missive forth.
Then learned that lost one all the truth. That sage
Confessed by miracles, that prophet vouched
By warnings old, that seer by words of might
Subduing all things to himself - that priest,
None other was than the uncomplaining boy
Five years his slave and swineherd! In him rage
Burst forth, with fear commixed, as when a beast
Strains in the toils. "Can I alone stand firm?"
He mused; and next, "Shall I, in mine old age,
Byword become - the vassal of my slave?
Shall I not rather drive him from my door
With wolf hounds and a curse?" As thus he stood
He marked the gifts, and bade men bare them in,
And homeward signed the messengers unfed.

But Milcho slept not all that night for thought,
And, forth ere sunrise issuing, paced a moor
Stone-roughened like the graveyard of dead hosts,
Till noontide. Sudden then he stopt, and thus
Discoursed within: "A plot from first to last,
The fraudulent bondage, flight, and late return;
For now I mind me of a foolish dream
Chance-sent, yet drawn by him awry. One night
Methought that boy from far hills drenched in rain
Dashed through my halls, all fire. From hands and head,

From hair and mouth, forth rushed a flaming fire
White, like white light, and still that mighty flame
Into itself took all. With hands outstretched
I spurned it. On my cradled daughters twain
It turned, and they were ashes. Then in burst
The south wind through the portals of the house,
Tempest rose-sweet, and blew those ashes forth
Wide as the realm. At dawn I sought the knave;
He glossed my vision thus: 'That fire is Faith -
Faith in the God Triune, the God made Man,
Sole light wherein I walk, and walking burn;
And they that walk with me shall burn like me
By Faith. But thou that radiance wilt repel,
Housed through ill-will, in Error's endless night.
Not less thy little daughters shall believe
With glory and great joy; and, when they die,
Report of them, like ashes blown abroad,
Shall light far lands, and health to men of Faith
Stream from their dust.' I drave the impostor forth:
Perjured ere long he fled, and now returns
To reap a harvest from his master's dream" -
Thus mused he, while black shadow swept the moor.
So day by day darker was Milcho's heart,
Till, with the endless brooding on one thought,
Began a little flaw within that brain
Whose strength was still his boast. Was no friend nigh?
Alas! what friend had he? All men he scorned;
Knew truly none. In each, the best and sweetest
Near him had ever pined, like stunted growth
Dwarfed by some glacier nigh. The fifth day dawned:
And inly thus he muttered, darkly pale:
"Five days; in three the messengers returned:
In three - in two - the Accursèd will be here,
Or blacken yonder Sleemish with his crew
Descending. Then those idiots, kerne and slave -
The mighty flame into itself takes all -
Full swarm will fly to meet him! Fool! fool! fool!
The man hath snared me with those gifts he sent;
Else had I barred the mountains: now 'twere late,
My people in revolt. Whole weeks his horde

Will throng my courts, demanding board and bed,
With hosts by Dichu sent to flout my pang,
And sorer make my charge. My granaries sacked,
My larder lean as ship six months ice-bound,
The man I hate will rise, and open shake
The invincible banner of his mad new Faith,
Till all that hear him shout, like winds or waves,
Belief; and I be left sole recusant;
Or else perhaps that Fury who prevails
At times o'er knee-joints of reluctant men,
By magic imped, may crumble into dust
By force my disbelief."

He raised his head,
And lo, before him lay the sea far ebbed
Sad with a sunset all but gone: the reeds
Sighed in the wind, and sighed a sweeter voice
Oft heard in childhood - now the last time heard:
"Believe!" it whispered. Vain the voice! That hour,
Stirred from the abyss, the sins of all his life
Around him rose like night - not one, but all -
That earliest sin which, like a dagger, pierced
His mother's heart; that worst, when summer drouth
Parched the brown vales, and infants thirsting died,
While from full pail he gorged his swine with milk
And flung the rest away. Sin-walled he stood:
God's Angels could not pierce that cincture dread,
Nor he look through it. Yet he dreamed he saw:
His life he saw; its labours, and its gains
Hard won, long-waited, wonder of his foes;
The manifold conquests of a Will oft tried;
Victory, Defeat, Retrieval; last, that scene
Around him spread: the wan sea and grey rocks;
And he was 'ware that on that self-same ledge
He, Milcho, thirty years gone by, had stood,
While pirates pushed to sea, leaving forlorn
On that wild shore a scared and weeping boy,
(His price two yearling kids and half a sheep)
Thenceforth his slave.

Not sole he mused that hour.
The Demon of his House beside him stood
Upon that iron coast, and whispered thus:
"Masterful man art thou for wit and strength;
Yet girl-like standst thou brooding! Weave a snare!
He comes for gold, this prophet. All thou hast
Heap in thy house; then fire it! In far lands
Build thee new fortunes. Frustrate thus shall he
Stare but on stones, his destined vassal scaped."

So fell the whisper; and as one who hears
And does, the stiff-necked man obsequious bent
His strong will to a stronger, and returned,
And gave command to heap within his house
His stored up wealth - yea, all things that were his -
Borne from his ships and granaries. It was done.
Then filled he his huge hall with resinous beams
Seasoned for far sea-voyage, and the ribs
Of ocean-sundering vessels deep in sea;
Which ended, to his topmost tower he clomb,
And therein sat two days, with face to south,
Clutching a brand; and oft through clenched teeth hissed,
Hissed long, "Because I will to disbelieve."
But ere the second sunset two brief hours,
Where comfortless leaned forth that western ridge
Long patched with whiteness by half melted snows,
There crept a gradual shadow. Soon the man
Discerned its import. There they hung - he saw them -
That company detested; hung as when
Storm-boding cloud on mountain hangs half way
Scarce moving, and in fear the shepherd cries,
"Would that the worse were come!" So dread to him
Those Heralds of fair Peace! He gazed upon them
With blood-shot eyes; a moment passed: he stood
Sole in his never festal hall, and flung
His lighted brand into that pile far forth,
And smiled that smile men feared to see, and turned,
And issuing faced the circle of his serfs
That wondering gathered round in thickening mass,
Eyeing that unloved House.

His place he chose
Beside that blighted ash, fronting those towers
Palled with red smoke, and muttered low, "So be it!
Worse to be vassal to the man I hate,"
With hueless lips. His whole white face that hour
Was scorched; and blistered was the dead tree's bark;
Yet there he stood; and in that fiery light
His life, no more triumphant, passed once more
In underthought before him, while on spread
The swift, contagious madness of that fire,
And muttered thus, not knowing it, the man,
"The mighty flame into itself takes all,"
Mechanic iteration. Not alone
Stood he that hour. The Demon of his House
By him once more and closer than of old,
Stood, whispering thus, "Thy game is now played out;
Henceforth a byword art thou - rich in youth -
Self-beggared in old age." And as the wind
Of that shrill whisper cut his listening soul,
The blazing roof fell in on all his wealth,
Hard-won, long-waited, wonder of his foes;
And, loud as laughter from ten thousand fiends,
Up rushed the fire. With arms outstretched he stood;
Stood firm; then forward with a wild beast's cry
He dashed himself into that terrible flame,
And vanished as a leaf.

Upon a spur
Of Sleemish, eastward on its northern slope,
Stood Patrick and his brethren, travel-worn,
When distant o'er the brown and billowy moor
Rose the white smoke, that changed ere long to flame,
From site unknown; for by the seaward crest
That keep lay hidden. Hands to forehead raised,
Wondering they watched it. One to other spake:
"The huge Dalriad forest is afire
Ere melted are the winter's snows!" Another,
"In vengeance o'er the ocean Creithe or Pict,
Favoured by magic, or by mist, have crossed,

And fired old Milcho's ships." But Patrick leaned
Upon his crosier, pale as the ashes wan
Left by a burned out city. Long he stood
Silent, till, sudden, fiercelier soared the flame
Reddening the edges of a cloud low hung;
And, after pause, vibration slow and stern
Troubling the burthened bosom of the air,
Upon a long surge of the northern wind
Came up - a murmur as of wintry seas
Far borne at night. All heard that sound; all felt it;
One only know its import. Patrick turned;
"The deed is done: the man I would have saved
Is dead, because he willed to disbelieve."

Yet Patrick grieved for Milcho, nor that hour
Passed further north. Three days on Sleemish hill
He dwelt in prayer. To Tara's royal halls
Then turned he, and subdued the royal house
And host to Christ, save Erin's king, Laeghaire.
But Milcho's daughters twain to Christ were born
In baptism, and each Emeria named:
Like rose-trees in the garden of the Lord
Grew they and flourished. Dying young, one grave
Received them at Cluanbrain. Healing thence
To many from their relics passed; to more
The spirit's happier healing, Love and Faith.

SAINT PATRICK AT TARA

The King is wroth with a greater wrath
Than the wrath of Nial or the wrath of Conn!
From his heart to his brow the blood makes path,
And hangs there, a red cloud, beneath his crown.

Is there any who knows not, from south to north,
That Laeghaire to-morrow his birthday keeps?
No fire may be lit upon hill or hearth
Till the King's strong fire in its kingly mirth
Up rushes from Tara's palace steeps!

Yet Patrick has lighted his Paschal fire
At Slane - it is holy Saturday -
And blessed his font 'mid the chaunting choir!
From hill to hill the flame makes way;
While the king looks on it his eyes with ire
Flash red, like Mars, under tresses grey.

The chiefs and the captains with drawn swords rose:
To avenge their Lord and the Realm they swore;
The Druids rose and their garments tore;
"The strangers to us and our Gods are foes!"
Then the king to Patrick a herald sent,
Who spake, 'Come up at noon and show
Who lit thy fire and with what intent:
These things the great king Laeghaire would know."

But Laeghaire had hid twelve men by the way,
Who swore by the sun the Saint to slay.

When the waters of Boyne began to bask
And fields to flash in the rising sun
The Apostle Evangelist kept his Pasch,
And Erin her grace baptismal won:
Her birthday it was: his font the rock,

He blessed the land, and he blessed his flock.

Then forth to Tara he fared full lowly:
The Staff of Jesus was in his hand:
Twelve priests paced after him chaunting slowly,
Printing their steps on the dewy land.
It was the Resurrection morn;
The lark sang loud o'er the springing corn;
The dove was heard, and the hunter's horn.

The murderers twelve stood by on the way;
Yet they saw nought save the lambs at play.

A trouble lurked in the monarch's eye
When the guest he counted for dead drew nigh:
He sat in state at his palace gate;
His chiefs and nobles were ranged around;
The Druids like ravens smelt some far fate;
Their eyes were gloomily bent on the ground.
Then spake Laeghaire: "He comes - beware!
Let none salute him, or rise from his chair!"

Like some still vision men see by night,
Mitred, with eyes of serene command,
Saint Patrick moved onward in ghostly white:
The Staff of Jesus was in his hand;
Twelve priests paced after him unafraid,
And the boy, Benignus, more like a maid;
Like a maid just wedded he walked and smiled,
To Christ new plighted, that priestly child.

They entered the circle; their anthem ceased;
The Druids their eyes bent earthward still:
On Patrick's brow the glory increased
As a sunrise brightening some sea-beat hill.
The warriors sat silent: strange awe they felt:
The chief bard, Dubtach, rose and knelt:

Then Patrick discoursed of the things to be
When time gives way to eternity,

Of kingdoms that fall, which are dreams not things,
And the Kingdom built by the King of kings.
Of Him he spake who reigns from the Cross;
Of the death which is life, and the life which is loss;
How all things were made by the Infant Lord,
And the small hand the Magian kings adored.
His voice sounded on like a throbbing flood
That swells all night from some far-off wood,
And when it ended - that wondrous strain -
Invisible myriads breathed "Amen!"

While he spake, men say that the refluent tide
On the shore by Colpa ceased to sink:
They say that the white stag by Mulla's side
O'er the green marge bending forbore to drink:
That the Brandon eagle forgat to soar;
That no leaf stirred in the wood by Lee:
Such stupor hung the island o'er,
For none might guess what the end would be.

Then whispered the king to a chief close by,
"It were better for me to believe than die!"

Yet the king believed not; but ordinance gave
That whoso would might believe that word:
So the meek believed, and the wise, and brave,
And Mary's Son as their God adored.
And the Druids, because they could answer nought,
Bowed down to the Faith the stranger brought.
That day on Erin God poured His Spirit:
Yet none like the chief of the bards had merit,
Dubtach! He rose and believed the first,
Ere the great light yet on the rest had burst.

SAINT PATRICK AND THE TWO PRINCESSES

FEDELM "THE RED ROSE," AND ETHNA "THE FAIR"

Like two sister fawns that leap,
Borne, as though on viewless wings,
Down bosky glade and ferny steep
To quench their thirst at silver springs,
From Cruachan palace through gorse and heather,
Raced the Royal Maids together.
Since childhood thus the twain had rushed
Each morn to Clebach's fountain-cell
Ere earliest dawn the East had flushed
To bathe them in its well:
Each morn with joy their young hearts tingled;
Each morn as, conquering cloud or mist,
The first beam with the wavelet mingled,
Mouth to mouth they kissed!

They stand by the fount with their unlooped hair -
A hand each raises - what see they there?
A white Form seated on Clebach stone;
A kinglike presence: the monks stood nigh:
Fronting the dawn he sat alone;
On the star of morning he fixed his eye:
That crozier he grasped shone bright; but brighter
The sunrise flashed from Saint Patrick's mitre!
They gazed without fear. To a kingdom dear
From the day of their birth those Maids had been;
Of wrong they had heard; but it came not near;
They hoped they were dear to the Power unseen.
They knelt when that Vision of Peace they saw;
Knelt, not in fear, but in loving awe:
The "Red Rose" bloomed like that East afar;
The "Fair One" shone like that morning star.

Then Patrick rose: no word he said,
But thrice he made the sacred Sign:
At the first, men say that the demons fled;
At the third flocked round them the Powers divine
Unseen. Like children devout and good,
Hands crossed on their bosoms, the maidens stood.

"Blessed and holy! This land is Eire:
Whence come ye to her, and the king our sire?"

"We come from a Kingdom far off yet near
Which the wise love well, and the wicked fear:
We come with blessing and come with ban,
We come from the Kingdom of God with man."

"Whose is that Kingdom? And say, therein
Are the chiefs all brave, and the maids all fair?
Is it clean from reptiles, and that thing, sin?
Is it like this kingdom of King Laeghaire?"

"The chiefs of that kingdom wage war on wrong,
And the clash of their swords is sweet as song;
Fair are the maids, and so pure from taint
The flash of their eyes turns sinner to saint;
There reptile is none, nor the ravening beast;
There light has no shadow, no end the feast."

"But say, at that feast hath the poor man place?
Is reverence there for the old head hoar?
For the cripple that never might join the race?
For the maimed that fought, and can fight no more?"

"Reverence is there for the poor and meek;
And the great King kisses the worn, pale cheek;
And the King's Son waits on the pilgrim guest;
And the Queen takes the little blind child to her breast:
There with a crown is the just man crowned;
But the false and the vengeful are branded and bound
In knots of serpents, and flung without pity
From the bastions and walls of the saintly City."

Then the eyes of the Maidens grew dark, as though
That judgment of God had before them passed:
And the two sweet faces grew dim with woe;
But the rose and the radiance returned at last.

"Are gardens there? Are there streams like ours?
Is God white-headed, or youthful and strong?
Hang there the rainbows o'er happy bowers?
Are there sun and moon and the thrush's song?"

"They have gardens there without noise or strife,
And there is the Tree of immortal Life:
Four rivers circle that blissful bound;
And Spirits float o'er it, and Spirits go round:
There, set in the midst, is the golden throne;
And the Maker of all things sits thereon:
A rainbow o'er-hangs him; and lo! therein
The beams are His Holy Ones washed from sin."

As he spake, the hearts of the Maids beat time
To music in heaven of peace and love;
And the deeper sense of that lore sublime
Came out from within them, and down from above;
By degrees came down; by degrees came out:
Who loveth, and hopeth, not long shall doubt.

"Who is your God? Is love on His brow?
Oh how shall we love Him and find Him? How?"
The pure cheek flamed like the dawn-touched dew:
There was silence: then Patrick began anew.
The princes who ride in your father's train
Have courted your love, but sued in vain; -
Look up, O Maidens; make answer free:
What boon desire you, and what would you be?"

"Pure we would be as yon wreath of foam,
Or the ripple which now yon sunbeams smite:
And joy we would have, and a songful home;
And one to rule us, and Love's delight."

"In love God fashioned whatever is,
The hills, and the seas, and the skiey fires;
For love He made them, and endless blis
Sustains, enkindles, uplifts, inspires:
That God is Father, and Son, and Spirit;
And the true and spotless His peace inherit:
And God made man, with his great sad heart,
That hungers when held from God apart.
Your sire is a King on earth: but I
Would mate you to One who is Lord on high:
There bride is maid: and her joy shall stand,
For the King's Son hath laid on her head His hand."
As he spake, the eyes of that lovely twain
Grew large with a tearful but glorious light,
Like skies of summer late cleared by rain,
When the full-orbed moon will be soon in sight.

"That Son of the King - is He fairest of men?
That mate whom He crowns - is she bright and blest?
Does she chase the red deer at His side through the glen?
Does she charm Him with song to His noontide rest?"

"That King's Son strove in a long, long war:
His people He freed; yet they wounded Him sore;
And still in His hands, and His feet, and His side,
The scars of His sorrow are 'graved, deep-dyed."

Then the breasts of the Maidens began to heave
Like harbour waves when beyond the bar
The great waves gather, and wet winds grieve,
And the roll of the tempest is heard afar.

"We will kiss, we will kiss those bleeding feet;
On the bleeding hands our tears shall fall;
And whatever on earth is dear or sweet,
For that wounded heart we renounce them all.

"Show us the way to His palace-gate:" -
"That way is thorny, and steep, and straight;
By none can His palace-gate be seen,

Save those who have washed in the waters clean."

They knelt; on their heads the wave he poured
Thrice in the name of the Triune Lord:
And he signed their brows with the Sign adored.
On Fedelm the "Red Rose," on Ethna "The Fair,"
God's dew shone bright in that morning air:
Some say that Saint Agnes, 'twixt sister and sister,
As the Cross touched each, bent over and kissed her.

Then sang God's new-born Creatures, "Behold!
We see God's City from heaven draw nigh:
But we thirst for the fountains divine and cold:
We must see the great King's Son, or die!
Come, Thou that com'st! Our wish is this,
That the body might die, and the soul, set free,
Swell out, like an infant's lips, to the kiss
Of the Lover who filleth infinity!"

"The City of God, by the water's grace,
Ye see: alone, they behold His Face,
Who have washed in the baths of Death their eyes,
And tasted His Eucharist Sacrifice."

"Give us the Sacrifice!" Each bright head
Bent toward it as sunflowers bend to the sun:
They ate; and the blood from the warm cheek fled:
The exile was over: the home was won:
A starry darkness o'erflowed their brain:
Far waters beat on some heavenly shore:
Like the dying away of a low, sweet strain,
The young life ebbed, and they breathed no more:
In death they smiled, as though on the breast
Of the Mother Maid they had found their rest.

The rumour spread: beside the bier
The King stood mute, and his chiefs and court:
The Druids dark-robed drew surlily near,
And the Bards storm-hearted, and humbler sort:
The "Staff of Jesus" Saint Patrick raised:

Angelic anthems above them swept:
There were that muttered; there were that praised:
But none who looked on that marvel wept.

For they lay on one bed, like Brides new-wed,
By Clebach well; and, the dirge days over,
On their smiling faces a veil was spread,
And a green mound raised that bed to cover.
Such were the ways of those ancient days -
To Patrick for aye that grave was given;
And above it he built a church in their praise;
For in them had Eire been spoused to heaven.

SAINT PATRICK AND THE CHILDREN OF FOCHLUT WOOD

Saint Patrick makes way into Fochlut wood by the sea, the oldest of Erin's forests, whence there had been borne unto him, then in a distant land, the Children's Wail from Erin. He meets there two young Virgins, who sing a dirge of man's sorrowful condition. Afterwards they lead him to the fortress of the king, their father. There are sung two songs, a song of Vengeance and a song of Lament; which ended, Saint Patrick makes proclamation of the Advent and of the Resurrection. The king and all his chiefs believe with full contentment.

One day as Patrick sat upon a stone
Judging his people, Pagan babes flocked round,
All light and laughter, angel-like of mien,
Sueing for bread. He gave it, and they ate:
Then said he, "Kneel;" and taught them prayer: but lo!
Sudden the stag hounds' music dinned the wind;
They heard; they sprang; they chased it. Patrick spake;
"It was the cry of children that I heard
Borne from the black wood o'er the midnight seas:
Where are those children? What avails though Kings
Have bowed before my Gospel, and in awe
Nations knelt low, unless I set mine eyes
On Fochlut Wood?" Thus speaking, he arose,
And, journeying with the brethren toward the West,
Fronted the confine of that forest old.

Then entered they that darkness; and the wood
Closed as a cavern round them. O'er its roof
Leaned roof of cloud, and hissing ran the wind,
And moaned the trunks for centuries hollowed out
Yet stalwart still. There, rooted in the rock,
Stood the huge growths, by us unnamed, that frowned
Perhaps on Partholan, the parricide,
When that first Pagan settler fugitive

Landed, a man foredoomed. Between the stems
The ravening beast now glared, now fled. Red leaves,
The last year's phantoms, rattled here and there.
The oldest wood that ever grew in Eire
Was Fochlut Wood, and gloomiest. Spirits of Ill
Made it their palace, and its labyrinths sowed
With poisons. Many a cave, with horrors thronged
Within it yawned, and many a chasm unseen
Waited the unwary treader. Cry of wolf
Pierced the cold air, and gibbering ghosts were heard;
And o'er the black marsh passed those wandering lights
That lure lost feet. A thousand pathways wound
From gloom to gloom. One only led to light:
That path was sharp with flints.

Then Patrick mused,
"O life of man, how dark a wood art thou!
Erring how many track thee till Despair,
Sad host, receives them in his crypt-like porch
At nightfall." Mute he paced. The brethren feared;
And fearing, knelt to God. Made strong by prayer
Westward once more they trod that dark, sharp way
Till deeper gloom announced the night, then slept
Guarded by angels. But the Saint all night
Watched, strong in prayer. The second day still on
They fared, like mariners o'er strange seas borne,
That keep in mist their soundings when the rocks
Vex the dark strait, and breakers roar unseen.
At last Benignus cried, "To God be praise!
He sends us better omens. See! the moss
Brightens the crag!" Ere long another spake:
"The worst is past! This freshness in the air
Wafts us a welcome from the great salt sea;
Fair spreads the fern: green buds are on the spray,
And violets throng the grass."

A few steps more
Brought them to where, with peaceful gleam, there spread
A forest pool that mirrored yew trees twain
With beads like blood-drops hung. A sunset flash

Kindled a glory in the osiers brown
Encircling that still water. From the reeds
A sable bird, gold-circled, slowly rose;
But when the towering tree-tops he outsoared,
Eastward a great wind swept him as a leaf.
Serenely as he rose a music soft
Swelled from afar; but, as that storm o'ertook him,
The music changed to one on-rushing note
O'ertaken by a second; both, ere long,
Blended in wail unending. Patrick's brow,
Listening that wail, was altered, and he spake:
"These were the Voices that I heard when stood
By night beside me in that southern land
God's angel, girt for speed. Letters he bare
Unnumbered, full of woes. He gave me one,
Inscribed, 'The Wailing of the Irish Race;'
And as I read that legend on mine ear
Forth from a mighty wood on Erin's coast
There rang the cry of children, 'Walk once more
Among us; bring us help!'" Thus Patrick spake:
Then towards that wailing paced with forward head.

Ere long they came to where a river broad,
Swiftly amid the dense trees winding, brimmed
The flower-enamelled marge, and onward bore
Green branches 'mid its eddies. On the bank
Two virgins stood. Whiter than earliest streak
Of matin pearl dividing dusky clouds
Their raiment; and, as oft in silent woods
White beds of wind-flower lean along the earth-breeze,
So on the river-breeze that raiment wan
Shivered, back blown. Slender they stood and tall,
Their brows with violets bound; while shone, beneath,
The dark blue of their never-tearless eyes.
Then Patrick, "For the sake of Him who lays
His blessing on the mourners, O ye maids,
Reveal to me your grief - if yours late sent,
Or sped in careless childhood." And the maids:
"Happy whose careless childhood 'scaped the wound:"
Then she that seemed the saddest added thus:

"Stranger! this forest is no roof of joy,
Nor we the only mourners; neither fall
Bitterer the widow's nor the orphan's tears
Now than of old; nor sharper than long since
That loss which maketh maiden widowhood.
In childhood first our sorrow came. One eve
Within our foster-parents' low-roofed house
The winter sunset from our bed had waned:
I slept, and sleeping dreamed. Beside the bed
There stood a lovely Lady crowned with stars;
A sword went through her heart. Down from that sword
Blood trickled on the bed, and on the ground.
Sorely I wept. The Lady spake: 'My child,
Weep not for me, but for thy country weep;
Her wound is deeper far than mine. Cry loud!
The cry of grief is Prayer.' I woke, all tears;
And lo! my little sister, stiff and cold,
Sat with wide eyes upon the bed upright:
That starry Lady with the bleeding heart
She, too, had seen, and heard her. Clamour vast
Rang out; and all the wall was fiery red;
And flame was on the sea. A hostile clan
Landing in mist, had fired our ships and town,
Our clansmen absent on a foray far,
And stricken many an old man, many a boy
To bondage dragged. Oh night with blood redeemed!
Upon the third day o'er the green waves rushed
The vengeance winged, with axe and torch, to quit
Wrong with new wrong, and many a time since then.
That night sad women on the sea sands toiled,
Drawing from wreck and ruin, beam or plank
To shield their babes. Our foster-parents slain,
Unheeded we, the children of the chief,
Roamed the great forest. There we told our dream
To children likewise orphaned. Sudden fear
Smote them as though themselves had dreamed that dream,
And back from them redoubled upon us;
Until at last from us and them rang out -
The dark wood heard it, and the midnight sea -
A great and bitter cry."

"That cry went up,
O children, to the heart of God; and He
Down sent it, pitying, to a far-off land,
And on into my heart. By that first pang
Which left the eternal pallor in your cheeks,
O maids, I pray you, sing once more that song
Ye sang but late. I heard its long last note:
Fain would I hear the song that such death died."

They sang: not scathless those that sing such song!
Grief, their instructress, of the Muses chief
To hearts by grief unvanquished, to their hearts
Had taught a melody that neither spared
Singer nor listener. Pale when they began,
Paler it left them. He not less was pale
Who, out of trance awaking, thanked them thus:
"Now know I of that sorrow in you fixed;
What, and how great it is, and bless that Power
Who called me forth from nothing for your sakes,
And sent me to this wood. Maidens, lead on!
A chieftain's daughters ye; and he, your sire,
And with him she who gave you your sweet looks
(Sadder perchance than you in songless age)
They, too, must hear my tidings. Once a Prince
Went solitary from His golden throne,
Tracking the illimitable wastes, to find
One wildered sheep, the meanest of the flock,
And on His shoulders bore it to that House
Where dwelt His Sire. 'Good Shepherd' was His Name.
My tidings these: heralds are we, footsore,
That bring the heart-sore comfort."

On they paced,
On by the rushing river without words.
Beside the elder sister Patrick walked,
Benignus by the younger. Fair her face;
Majestic his, though young. Her looks were sad
And awe-struck; his, fulfilled with secret joy,
Sent forth a gleam as when a morn-touched bay

Through ambush shines of woodlands. Soon they stood
Where sea and river met, and trod a path
Wet with salt spray, and drank the clement breeze,
And saw the quivering of the green gold wave,
And, far beyond, that fierce aggressor's bourn,
Fair haunt for savage race, a purple ridge
By rainy sunbeam gemmed from glen to glen,
Dim waste of wandering lights. The sun, half risen,
Lay half sea-couched. A neighbouring height sent forth
Welcome of baying hounds; and, close at hand,
They reached the chieftain's keep.

A white-haired man
And long since blind, there sat he in his hall,
Untamed by age. At times a fiery gleam
Flashed from his sightless eyes; and oft the red
Burned on his forehead, while with splenetic speech
Stirred by ill news or memory stung, he banned
Foes and false friend. Pleased by his daughters' tale,
At once he stretched his huge yet aimless hands
In welcome towards his guests. Beside him stood
His mate of forty years by that strong arm
From countless suitors won. Pensive her face:
With parted youth the confidence of youth
Had left her. Beauty, too, though with remorse,
Its seat had half relinquished on a cheek
Long time its boast, and on that willowy form,
So yielding now, where once in strength upsoared
The queenly presence. Tenderest grace not less
Haunted her life's dim twilight - meekness, love -
That humble love, all-giving, that seeks nought,
Self-reverent calm, and modesty in age.
She turned an anxious eye on him she loved;
And, bending, kissed at times that wrinkled hand,
By years and sorrows made his wife far more
Than in her nuptial bloom. These two had lost
Five sons, their hope, in war.

That eve it chanced
High feast was holden in the chieftain's tower

To solemnise his birthday. In they flocked,
Each after each, the warriors of the clan,
Not without pomp heraldic and fair state
Barbaric, yet beseeming. Unto each
Seat was assigned for deeds or lineage old,
And to the chiefs allied. Where each had place
Above him waved his banner. Not for this
Unhonoured were the pilgrim guests. They sat
Where, fed by pinewood and the seeded cone,
The loud hearth blazed. Bathed were the wearied feet
By maidens of the place and nurses grey,
And dried in linen fragrant still with flowers
Of years when those old nurses too were fair.
And now the board was spread, and carved the meat,
And jests ran round, and many a tale was told,
Some rude, but none opprobrious. Banquet done,
Page-led the harper entered, old, and blind:
The noblest ranged his chair, and spread the mat;
The loveliest raised his wine cup, one light hand
Laid on his shoulder, while the golden hair
Commingled with the silver. "Sing," they cried,
"The death of Deirdrè; or that desolate sire
That slew his son, unweeting; or that Queen
Who from her palace pacing with fixed eyes
Stared at those heads in dreadful circle ranged,
The heads of traitor-friends that slew her lord
Then mocked the friend they murdered. Leal and true,
The Bard who wrought that vengeance!" Thus he sang:

THE LAY OF THE HEADS

The Bard returns to a stricken house:
What shape is that he rears on high?
A withe of the Willow, set round with Heads:
They blot that evening sky.

A Widow meets him at the gates:
What fixes thus that Widow's eye?
She names the name; but she sees not the man,
Nor beyond him that reddening sky.

"Bard of the Brand, thou Foster-Sire
Of him they slew - their friend - my lord -
What Head is that - the first - that frowns
Like a traitor self-abhorred?"

"Daughter of Orgill wounded sore,
Thou of the fateful eye serene,
Fergus is he. The feast he made
That snared thy Cuchullene."

"What Head is that - the next - half-hid
In curls full lustrous to behold?
They mind me of a hand that once
I saw amid their gold."

"'Tis Manadh. He that by the shore
Held rule, and named the waves his steeds:
'Twas he that struck the stroke accursed -
Headless this day he bleeds."

"What Head is that close by - so still,
With half-closed lids, and lips that smile?
Methinks I know their voice: methinks
His wine they quaffed erewhile!"

"'Twas he raised high that severed head:
Thy head he raised, my Foster-Child!
That was the latest stroke I struck:
I struck that stroke, and smiled."

"What Heads are those - that twain, so like,
Flushed as with blood by yon red sky?"
"Each unto each, *his* Head they rolled;
Red on that grass they lie."

"That paler twain, which face the East?"
"Laegar is one; the other Hilt;
Silent they watched the sport! they share
The doom, that shared the guilt."

"Bard of the Vengeance! well thou knew'st
Blood cries for blood! O kind, and true,
How many, kith and kin, have died
That mocked the man they slew?"

"O Woman of the fateful eye,
The untrembling voice, the marble mould,
Seven hundred men, in house or field,
For the man they mocked, lie cold."

"Their wives, thou Bard? their wives? their wives?
Far off, or nigh, through Inisfail,
This hour what are they? Stand they mute
Like me; or make their wail?"

"O Eimer! women weep and smile;
The young have hope, the young that mourn;
But I am old; my hope was he:
He that can ne'er return!
"O Conal! lay me in his grave:
Oh! lay me by my husband's side:
Oh! lay my lips to his in death;"
She spake, and, standing, died.

She fell at last - in death she fell -

She lay, a black shade, on the ground;
And all her women o'er her wailed
Like sea-birds o'er the drowned.

Thus to the blind chief sang that harper blind,
Hymning the vengeance; and the great hall roared
With wrath of those wild listeners. Many a heel
Smote the rough stone in scorn of them that died
Not three days past, so seemed it! Direful hands,
Together dashed, thundered the Avenger's praise.
At last the tide of that fierce tumult ebbed
O'er shores of silence. From her lowly seat
Beside her husband's spake the gentle Queen:
"My daughters, from your childhood ye were still
A voice of music in your father's house -
Not wrathful music. Sing that song ye made
Or found long since, and yet in forest sing,
If haply Power Unknown may hear and help."
She spake, and at her word her daughters sang.

"Lost, lost, all lost! O tell us what is lost?
Behold, this too is hidden! Let him speak,
If any knows. The wounded deer can turn
And see the shaft that quivers in its flank;
The bird looks back upon its broken wing;
But we, the forest children, only know
Our grief is infinite, and hath no name.
What woman-prophet, shrouded in dark veil,
Whispered a Hope sadder than Fear? Long since,
What Father lost His children in the wood?
Some God? And can a God forsake? Perchance
His face is turned to nobler worlds new-made;
Perchance his palace owns some later bride
That hates the dead Queen's children, and with charm
Prevails that they are exiled from his eyes,
The exile's winter theirs - the exile's song.

"Blood, ever blood! The sword goes raging on
O'er hill and moor; and with it, iron-willed,
Drags on the hand that holds it and the man

To slake its ceaseless thirst for blood of men;
Fire takes the little cot beside the mere,
And leaps upon the upland village: fire
Up clambers to the castle on the crag;
And whom the fire has spared the hunger kills;
And earth draws all into her thousand graves.

"Ah me! the little linnet knows the branch
Whereon to build; the honey-pasturing bee
Knows the wild heath, and how to shape its cell;
Upon the poisonous berry no bird feeds;
So well their mother, Nature, helps her own.
Mothers forsake not; - can a Father hate?
Who knows but that He yearns - that Sire Unseen -
To clasp His children? All is sweet and sane,
All, all save man! Sweet is the summer flower,
The day-long sunset of the autumnal woods;
Fair is the winter frost; in spring the heart
Shakes to the bleating lamb. O then what thing
Might be the life secure of man with man,
The infant's smile, the mother's kiss, the love
Of lovers, and the untroubled wedded home?
This might have been man's lot. Who sent the woe?
Who formed man first? Who taught him first the ill way?
One creature, only, sins; and he the highest!

"O Higher than the highest! Thou Whose hand
Made us - Who shaped'st that hand Thou wilt not clasp,
The eye Thou open'st not, the sealed-up ear!
Be mightier than man's sin: for lo, how man
Seeks Thee, and ceases not: through noontide cave
And dark air of the dawn-unlighted peak
To Thee how long he strains the weak, worn eye
If haply he might see Thy vesture's hem
On farthest winds receding! Yea, how oft
Against the blind and tremulous wall of cliff
Tormented by sea surge, he leans his ear
If haply o'er it name of Thine might creep;
Or bends above the torrent-cloven abyss,
If falling flood might lisp it! Power unknown!

He hears it not: Thou hear'st his beating heart
That cries to Thee for ever! From the veil
That shrouds Thee, from the wood, the cloud, the void,
O, by the anguish of all lands evoked,
Look forth! Though, seeing Thee, man's race should die,
One moment let him see Thee! Let him lay
At least his forehead on Thy foot in death!"

So sang the maidens: but the warriors frowned;
And thus the blind king muttered, "Bootless weed
Is plaint where help is none!" But wives and maids
And the thick-crowding poor, that many a time
Had wailed on war-fields o'er their brethren slain,
Went down before that strain as river reeds
Before strong wind, went down when o'er them passed
Its last word, "Death;" and grief's infection spread
From least to first; and weeping filled the hall.
Then on Saint Patrick fell compassion great;
He rose amid that concourse, and with voice
And words now lost, alas, or all but lost,
Such that the chief of sight amerced, beheld
The imagined man before him crowned with light,
Proclaimed that God who hideth not His face,
His people's King and Father; open flung
The portals of His realm, that inward rolled,
With music of a million singing spheres
Commanded all to enter. Who was He
Who called the worlds from nought? His name is Love!
In love He made those worlds. They have not lost,
The sun his splendour, nor the moon her light:
That miracle survives. Alas for thee!
Thou better miracle, fair human love,
That splendour shouldst have been of home and hearth,
Now quenched by mortal hate! Whence come our woes
But from our lusts? O desecrated law
By God's own finger on our hearts engraved,
How well art thou avenged! No dream it was,
That primal greatness, and that primal peace:
Man in God's image at the first was made,
A God to rule below!

He told it all -
Creation, and that Sin which marred its face;
And how the great Creator, creature made,
God - God for man incarnate - died for man:
Dead, with His Cross he thundered on the gates
Of Death's blind Hades. Then, with hands outstretched
His Holy Ones that, in their penance prison
From hope in Him had ceased not, to the light
Flashed from His bleeding hands and branded brow
Through darkness soared: they reign with Him in heaven:
Their brethren we, the children of one Sire.
Long time he spake. The winds forbore their wail;
The woods were hushed. That wondrous tale complete,
Not sudden fell the silence; for, as when
A huge wave forth from ocean toiling mounts
High-arched, in solid bulk, the beach rock-strewn,
Burying his hoar head under echoing cliffs,
And, after pause, refluent to sea returns
Not all at once is stillness, countless rills
Or devious winding down the steep, or borne
In crystal leap from sea-shelf to sea-well,
And sparry grot replying; gradual thus
With lessening cadence sank that great discourse,
While round him gazed Saint Patrick, now the old
Regarding, now the young, and flung on each
In turn his boundless heart, and gazing longed
As only Apostolic heart can long
To help the helpless.

"Fair, O friends, the bourn
We dwell in! Holy King makes happy land:
Our King is in our midst. He gave us gifts;
Laws that are Love, the sovereignty of Truth.
What, sirs, ye knew Him not! But ye by signs
Foresaw His coming, as, when buds are red
Ye say, 'The spring is nigh us.' Him, unknown,
Each loved who loved his brother! Shepherd youths,
Who spread the pasture green beneath your lambs
And freshened it with snow-fed stream and mist?
Who but that Love unseen? Grey mariners,

Who lulled the rough seas round your midnight nets,
And sent the landward breeze? Pale sufferers wan,
Rejoice! His are ye; yea, and His the most!
Have ye not watched the eagle that upstirs
Her nest, then undersails her falling brood
And stays them on her plumes, and bears them up
Till, taught by proof, they learn their unguessed powers
And breast the storm? Thus God stirs up His people;
Thus proves by pain. Ye too, O hearths well-loved!
How oft your sin-stained sanctities ye mourned!
Wives! from the cradle reigns the Bethelem Babe!
Maidens! henceforth the Virgin Mother spreads
Her shining veil above you!

"Speak aloud,
Chieftains world-famed! I hear the ancient blood
That leaps against your hearts! What? Warriors ye!
Danger your birthright, and your pastime death!
Behold your foes! They stand before you plain:
Ill passions, base ambitions, falsehood, hate:
Wage war on these! A King is in your host!
His hands no roses plucked but on the Cross:
He came not hand of man in woman's tasks
To mesh. In woman's hand, in childhood's hand,
Much more in man's, He lodged His conquering sword;
Them too His soldiers named, and vowed to war.
Rise, clan of Kings, rise, champions of man's race,
Heaven's sun-clad army militant on earth,
One victory gained, the realm decreed is ours.
The bridal bells ring out, for Low with High
Is wed in endless nuptials. It is past,
The sin, the exile, and the grief. O man,
Take thou, renewed, thy sister-mate by hand;
Know well thy dignity, and hers: return,
And meet once more Thy Maker, for He walks
Once more within thy garden, in the cool
Of the world's eve!"

The words that Patrick spake
Were words of power, not futile did they fall:

But, probing, healed a sorrowing people's wound.
Round him they stood, as oft in Grecian days,
Some haughty city sieged, her penitent sons
Thronging green Pnyx or templed Forum hushed
Hung listening on that People's one true Voice,
The man that ne'er had flattered, ne'er deceived,
Nursed no false hope. It was the time of Faith;
Open was then man's ear, open his heart:
Pride spurned not then that chiefest strength of man
The power, by Truth confronted, to believe.
Not savage was that wild, barbaric race:
Spirit was in them. On their knees they sank,
With foreheads lowly bent; and when they rose
Such sound went forth as when late anchored fleet
Touched by dawn breeze, shakes out its canvas broad
And sweeps into new waters. Man with man
Clasped hands; and each in each a something saw
Till then unseen. As though flesh-bound no more,
Their souls had touched. One Truth, the Spirit's life,
Lived in them all, a vast and common joy.
And yet as when, that Pentecostal morn,
Each heard the Apostle in his native tongue,
So now, on each, that Truth, that Joy, that Life
Shone forth with beam diverse. Deep peace to one
Those tidings seemed, a still vale after storm;
To one a sacred rule, steadying the world;
A third exulting saw his youthful hope
Written in stars; a fourth triumphant hailed
The just cause, long oppressed. Some laughed, some wept:
But she, that aged chieftain's mournful wife
Clasped to her boding breast his hoary head
Loud clamouring, "Death is dead; and not for long
That dreadful grave can part us." Last of all,
He too believed. That hoary head had shaped
Full many a crafty scheme: - behind them all
Nature held fast her own.

O happy night!
Back through the gloom of centuries sin-defaced
With what a saintly radiance thou dost shine!

They slept not, on the loud-resounding shore
In glory roaming. Many a feud that night
Lay down in holy grave, or, mockery made,
Was quenched in its own shame. Far shone the fires
Crowning dark hills with gladness: soared the song;
And heralds sped from coast to coast to tell
How He the Lord of all, no Power Unknown
But like a man rejoicing in his house,
Ruled the glad earth. That demon-haunted wood,
Sad Erin's saddest region, yet, men say,
Tenderest for all its sadness, rang at last
With hymns of men and angels. Onward sailed
High o'er the long, unbreaking, azure waves
A mighty moon, full-faced, as though on winds
Of rapture borne. With earliest red of dawn
Northward once more the wingèd war-ships rushed
Swift as of old to that long hated shore -
Not now with axe and torch. His Name they bare
Who linked in one the nations.

On a cliff
Where Fochlut's Wood blackened the northern sea
A convent rose. Therein those sisters twain
Whose cry had summoned Patrick o'er the deep,
Abode, no longer weepers. Pallid still,
In radiance now their faces shone; and sweet
Their psalms amid the clangour of rough brine.
Ten years in praise to God and good to men
That happy precinct housed them. In their morn
Grief had for them her great work perfected;
Their eve was bright as childhood. When the hour
Came for their blissful transit, from their lips
Pealed forth ere death that great triumphant chant
Sung by the Virgin Mother. Ages passed;
And, year by year, on wintry nights, *that* song
Alone the sailors heard - a cry of joy.

SAINT PATRICK AND KING LAEGHAIRE

"Thou son of Calphurn, in peace go forth!
This hand shall slay them whoe'er shall slay thee!
The carles shall stand to their necks in earth
Till they die of thirst who mock or stay thee!

"But my father, Nial, who is dead long since,
Permits not me to believe thy word;
For the servants of Jesus, thy heavenly Prince,
Once dead, lie flat as in sleep, interred:
But we are as men that through dark floods wade;
We stand in our black graves undismayed;
Our faces are turned to the race abhorred,
And at each hand by us stand spear or sword,
Ready to strike at the last great day,
Ready to trample them back into clay!

"This is my realm, and men call it Eire,
Wherein I have lived and live in hate
Like Nial before me and Erc his sire,
Of the race Lagenian, ill-named the Great!"

Thus spake Laeghaire, and his host rushed on,
A river of blood as yet unshed: -
At noon they fought: and at set of sun
That king lay captive, that host lay dead!

The Lagenian loosed him, but bade him swear
He would never demand of them Tribute more:
So Laeghaire by the dread "God-Elements" swore,
By the moon divine and the earth and air;
He swore by the wind and the broad sunshine
That circle for ever both land and sea,
By the long-backed rivers, and mighty wine,
By the cloud far-seeing, by herb and tree,

By the boon spring shower, and by autumn's fan,
By woman's breast, and the head of man,
By Night and the noonday Demon he swore
He would claim the Boarian Tribute no more.

But with time wrath waxed; and he brake his faith:
Then the dread "God-Elements" wrought his death;
For the Wind and Sun-Strength by Cassi's side
Came down and smote on his head that he died.
Death-sick three days on his throne he sate;
Then died, as his father died, great in hate.

They buried their king upon Tara's hill,
In his grave upright - there stands he still:
Upright there stands he as men that wade
By night through a castle-moat, undismayed;
On his head is the crown, the spear in his hand;
And he looks to the hated Lagenian land.

Such rites in the time of wrath and wrong
Were Eire's: baptised, they were hers no longer:
For Patrick had taught her his sweet new song,
"Though hate is strong, yet love is stronger."

SAINT PATRICK AND THE IMPOSTOR; OR, MAC KYLE OF MAN

Mac Kyle, a child of death, dwells in a forest with other men like unto himself, that slay whom they will. Saint Patrick coming to that wood, a certain Impostor devises how he may be deceived and killed; but God smites the Impostor through his own snare, and he dies. Mac Kyle believes, and demanding penance is baptised. Afterwards he preaches in Manann [1] Isle, and becomes a great Saint.

In Uladh, near Magh Inis, lived a chief,
Fierce man and fell. From orphaned childhood he
Through lawless youth to blood-stained middle age
Had rushed as stormy morn to stormier noon,
Working, except that still he spared the poor,
All wrongs with iron will; a child of death.
Thus spake he to his followers, while the woods
Snow-cumbered creaked, their scales of icy mail
Angered by winter winds: "At last he comes,
He that deceives the people with great signs,
And for the tinkling of a little gold
Preaches new Gods. Where rises yonder smoke
Beyond the pinewood, camps this Lord of Dupes:
How say ye? Shall he track o'er Uladh's plains,
As o'er the land beside, his venomous way?
Forth with your swords! and if that God he serves
Can save him, let him prove it!"

Dark with wrath
Thus spake Mac Kyle; and all his men approved,
Shouting, while downward fell the snows hard-caked Loosened by shock of forest-echoed hands,
Save Garban. Crafty he, and full of lies,
That thing which Patrick hated. Sideway first

---

[1] The Isle of Man.

Glancing, as though some secret foe were nigh,
He spake: "Mac Kyle! a counsel for thine ear!
A man of counsel I, as thou of war!
The people love this stranger. Patrick slain,
Their wrath will blaze against us, and demand
An *eric* for his head. Let us by craft
Unravel first *his* craft: then safe our choice;
We slay a traitor, or great ransom take:
Impostors lack not gold. Lay me as dead
Upon a bier: above me spread yon cloth,
And make your wail: and when the seer draws nigh
Worship him, crying, 'Lo, our friend is dead!
Kneel, prophet, kneel, and pray that God thou serv'st
To raise him.' If he kneels, no prophet he,
But like the race of mortals. Sweep the cloth
Straight from my face; then, laughing, I will rise."

Thus counselled Garban; and the counsel pleased;
Yet pleased not God. Upon a bier, branch-strewn,
They laid their man, and o'er him spread a cloth;
Then, moving towards that smoke behind the pines,
They found the Saint and brought him to that bier,
And made their moan - and Garban 'neath that cloth
Smiled as he heard it - "Lo, our friend is dead!
Great prophet kneel; and pray the God thou serv'st
To raise him from the dead."

The man of God
Upon them fixed a sentence-speaking eye:
"Yea! he is dead. In this ye have not lied:
Behold, this day shall Garban's covering be
The covering of the dead. Remove that cloth."

Then drew they from his face the cloth; and lo!
Beneath it Garban lay, a corpse stone-cold.

Amazement fell upon that bandit throng,
Contemplating that corpse, and on Mac Kyle
Grief for his friend, remorse, and strong belief,
A threefold power: for she that at his birth,

Her brief life faithful to that Law she knew,
Had died, in region where desires are crowned
That hour was strong in prayer. "From God he came,"
Thus cried they; "and we worked a work accursed,
Tempting God's prophet." Patrick heard, and spake;
"Not me ye tempted, but the God I serve."
At last Mac Kyle made answer: "I have sinned;
I, and this people, whom I made to sin:
Now therefore to thy God we yield ourselves
Liegemen henceforth, his thralls as slave to Lord,
Or horse to master. That which thou command'st
That will we do." And Patrick said, "Believe;
Confess your sins; and be baptised to God,
The Father, and the Son, and Holy Spirit,
And live true life." Then Patrick where he stood
Above the dead, with hands uplifted preached
To these in anguish and in terror bowed
The tidings of great joy from Bethlehem's Crib
To Calvary's Cross. Sudden upon his knees,
Heart-pierced, as though he saw that Head thorn-pierced,
Fell that wild chief, and was baptised to God;
And, lifting up his great strong hands, while still
The waters streamed adown his matted locks,
He cried, "Alas, my master, and my sire!
I sinned a mighty sin; for in my heart
Fixed was my purpose, soon as thou hadst knelt,
To slay thee with my sword. Therefore judge thou
What *eric* I must pay to quit my sin?"
Him Patrick answered, "God shall be thy Judge:
Arise, and to the seaside flee, as one
That flies his foe. There shalt thou find a boat
Made of one hide: eat nought, and nothing take
Except one cloak alone: but in that boat
Sit thou, and bear the sin-mark on thy brow,
Facing the waves, oarless and rudderless;
And bind the boat chain thrice around thy feet,
And fling the key with strength into the main,
Far as thou canst: and wheresoe'er the breath
Of God shall waft thee, there till death abide
Working the Will Divine." Then spake that chief,

"I, that commanded others, can obey;
Such lore alone is mine: but for this man
That sinned my sin, alas, to see him thus!"
To whom the Saint, "For him, when thou art gone,
My prayer shall rise. If God will raise the dead
He knows: not I."

Then rose that chief, and rushed
Down to the shore, as one that flies his foe;
Nor ate, nor drank, nor spake to wife or child,
But loosed a little boat, of one hide made,
And sat therein, and round his ankles wound
The boat chain thrice; and flung the key far forth
Above the ridged sea foam. The Lord of all
Gave ordinance to the wind, and, as a leaf
Swift rushed that boat, oarless and rudderless,
Over the on-shouldering, broad-backed, glaucous wave
Slow-rising like the rising of a world,
And purple wastes beyond, with funeral plume
Crested, a pallid pomp. All night the chief
Under the roaring tempest heard the voice
That preached the Son of Man; and when the morn
Shone out, his coracle drew near the surge
Reboant on Manann's Isle. Not unbeheld
Rose it, and fell; not unregarded danced
A black spot on the inrolling ridge, then hung
Suspense upon the mile-long cataract
That, overtoppling, changed grass-green to light,
And drowned the shores in foam. Upon the sands
Two white-haired Elders in the salt air knelt,
Offering to God their early orisons,
Coninri and Romael. Sixty years
These two unto a hard and stubborn race
Had preached the Word; and gaining by their toil
But thirty souls, had daily prayed their God
To send ere yet they died some ampler arm,
And reap the ill-grown harvest of their youth.
Ten years they prayed, not doubting, and from God,
Who hastens not, this answer had received,
"Ye shall not die until ye see his face."

Therefore, each morning, peered they o'er the waves,
Long-watching. These through breakers dragged the man,
Their wished-for prize, half-frozen, and nigh to death,
And bare him to their cell, and warmed and fed him,
And heaped his couch with skins. Deep sleep he slept
Till evening lay upon the level sea
With roses strewn like bridal chamber's floor;
Within it one star shone. Rested, he woke
And sought the shore. From earth, and sea, and sky,
Then passed into his spirit the Spirit of Love;
And there he vowed his vow, fierce chief no more,
But soldier of the cross.

The weeks ran on,
And daily those grey Elders ministered
God's teaching to that chief, demanding still,
"Son, understandst thou? Gird thee like a man
To clasp, and hold, the total Faith of Christ,
And give us leave to die." The months fled fast:
Ere violets bloomed, he knew the creed; and when
Far heathery hills purpled the autumnal air,
He sang the psalter whole. That tale he told
Had power, and Patrick's name. His strenous arm
Labouring with theirs, reaped harvest heavy and sound,
Till wondering gazed their wearied eyes on barns
Knee-deep in grain. At last an eve there fell,
When, on the shore in commune, with such might
Discoursed that pilgrim of the things of God,
Such insight calm, and wisdom reverence-born,
Each on the other gazing in their hearts
Received once more an answer from the Lord,
"Now is your task completed: ye shall die."

Then on the red sand knelt those Elders twain
With hands upraised, and all their hoary hair
Tinged like the foam-wreaths by that setting sun,
And sang their "Nunc Dimittis." At its close
High on the sandhills, 'mid the tall hard grass
That sighed eternal o'er the unbounded waste
With ceaseless yearnings like their own for death

They found the place where first, that bark descried,
Their sighs were changed to songs. That spot they marked,
And said, "Our resurrection place is here:"
And, on the third day dying, in that place
The man who loved them laid them, at their heads
Planting one cross because their hearts were one
And one their lives. The snowy-breasted bird
Of ocean o'er their undivided graves
Oft flew with wailing note; but they rejoiced
'Mid God's high realm glittering in endless youth.

These two with Christ, on him, their son in Christ
Their mantle fell; and strength to him was given.
Long time he toiled alone; then round him flocked
Helpers from far. At last, by voice of all
He gat the Island's great episcopate,
And king-like ruled the region. This is he,
Mac Kyle of Uladh, bishop, and Penitent,
Saint Patrick's missioner in Manann's Isle,
Sinner one time, and, after sinner, Saint
World-famous. May his prayer for sinners plead!

SAINT PATRICK AT CASHEL; OR, THE BAPTISM OF AENGUS

Saint Patrick goes to Cashel of the Rings to celebrate the Feast of the Annunciation. Aengus, who reigns there, receives him with all honour. He and his people believe, and by Baptism are added unto the Church. Aengus desires to resign his sovereignty, and become a monk. The Saint suffers not this, because he had discovered by two notable signs, both at the baptism of Aengus and before it, that the Prince is of those who are called by God to rule men.

When Patrick now o'er Ulster's forest bound,
And Connact, echoing to the western wave,
And Leinster, fair with hill-suspended woods,
Had raised the cross, and where the deep night ruled,
Splendour had sent of everlasting light,
Sole peace of warring hearts, to Munster next,
Thomond and Desmond, Heber's portion old,
He turned; and, fired by love that mocks at rest
Pushed on through raging storm the whole night long,
Intent to hold the Annunciation Feast
At Cashel of the Kings. The royal keep
High-seated on its Rock, as morning broke
Faced them at last; and at the selfsame hour
Aengus, in his father's absence lord,
Rising from happy sleep and heaven-sent dreams
Went forth on duteous tasks. With sudden start
The prince stept back; for, o'er the fortress court
Like grove storm-levelled lay the idols huge,
False gods and foul that long had awed the land,
Prone, without hand of man. O'er-awed he gazed;
Then on the air there rang a sound of hymns,
And by the eastern gate Saint Patrick stood,
The brethren round him. On their shaggy garb
Auroral mist, struck by the rising sun,
Glittered, that diamond-panoplied they seemed,

And as a heavenly vision. At that sight
The youth, descending with a wildered joy,
Welcomed his guests: and, ere an hour, the streets
Sparkled far down like flowering meads in spring,
So thronged the folk in holiday attire
To see the man far-famed. "Who spurns our gods?"
Once they had cried in wrath: but, year by year,
Tidings of some deliverance great and strange,
Some life more noble, some sublimer hope,
Some regal race enthroned beyond the grave,
Had reached them from afar. The best believed,
Great hearts for whom nor earthly love sufficed
Nor earthly fame. The meaner scoffed: yet all
Desired the man. Delay had edged their thirst.

Then Patrick, standing up among them, spake,
And God was with him. Not as when loose tongue
Babbles vain rumour, or the Sophist spins
Thought's air-hung cobwebs gay with Fancy's dews,
Spake he, but words of might, as when a man
Bears witness to the things which he has seen,
And tells of that he knows: and as the harp
Attested is by rapture of the ear,
And sunlight by consenting of the eye
That, seeing, knows it sees, and neither craves
Inferior demonstration, so his words
Self-proved, went forth and conquered: for man's mind,
Created in His image who is Truth,
Challenged by truth, with recognising voice
Cries out "Flesh of my flesh, bone of my bone,"
And cleaves thereto. In all that listening host
One vast, dilating heart yearned to its God.
Then burst the bond of years. No haunting doubt
They knew. God dropped on them the robe of Truth
Sun-like: down fell the many-coloured weed
Of error; and, reclothed ere yet unclothed,
They walked a new-born earth. The blinded Past
Fled, vanquished. Glorious more than strange it seemed
That He who fashioned man should come to man,
And raise by ruling. They, His trumpet heard,

In glory spurned demons misdeemed for gods:
The great chief had returned: the clan enthralled
Trod down the usurping foe.

Then rose the cry,
"Join us to Christ!" His strong eyes on them set,
Patrick replied, "Know ye what thing ye seek
Ye that would fain be house-mates with my King?
Ye seek His cross!" He paused, then added slow:
"If ye be liegeful, sirs, decree the day,
His baptism shall be yours."

That eve, while shone
The sunset on the green-touched woods, that, grazed
By onward flight of unalighting spring,
Caught warmth yet scarcely flamed, Aengus stood
With Patrick in a westward-facing tower
Which overlooked far regions town-besprent,
And lit with winding waters. Thus he spake:
"My Father! what is sovereignty of man?
Say, can I shield yon host from death, from sin,
Taking them up into my breast, like God?
I trow not so! Mine be the lowliest place
Following thy King who left his Father's throne
To walk the lowliest!" Patrick answered thus:
"Best lot thou choosest, son. If thine that lot
Thou know'st not yet; nor I. The Lord, thy God,
Will teach us."

When the day decreed had dawned
Loud rang the bull-horn; and on every breeze
Floated the banners, saffron, green, and blue;
While issuing from the horizon's utmost verge
The full-voiced People flocked. So swarmed of old
Some migratory nation, instinct-urged
To fly their native wastes sad winter's realm;
So thronged on southern slopes when, far below,
Shone out the plains of promise. Bright they came!
No summer sea could wear a blithsomer sheen
Though every dancing crest and milky plume

Ran on with rainbows braided. Minstrel songs
Wafted like winds those onward hosts, or swayed
Or stayed them; while among them heralds passed
Lifting white wands of office. Foremost rode
Aileel, the younger brother of the prince:
He ruled a milk-white horse. Fluttered, breeze-borne
His mantle green, while all his golden hair
Streamed back redundant from the ring of gold
Circling his head uncovered. Loveliest light
Of innocence and joy was on that face:
Full well the young maids marked it! Brighter yet
Beamed he, his brother noting. On the verge
Of Cashel's Rock that hour Aengus stood,
By Patrick's side. That concourse nearer now
He gazed upon it, crying, with clasped hands,
"My Father, fair is sunrise, fair the sea,
The hills, the plains, the wind-stirred wood, the maid;
But what is like a People onward borne
In gladness? When I see that sight, my heart
Expands like palace-gates wide open flung
That say to all men, 'Enter.'" Then the Saint
Laid on that royal head a hand of might,
And said, "The Will of God decrees thee King!
Son of this People art thou: Sire one day
Thou shalt be! Son and Sire in one are King.
Shepherd for God thy flock, thou Shepherd true!"
He spake: that word was ratified in Heaven.

Meantime that multitude innumerable
Had reached the Rock, and, now the winding road
In pomp ascending, faced those fair-wrought gates
Which, by the warders at the prince's sign
Drawn back, to all gave entrance. In they streamed,
Filling the central courtway. Patrick stood
High stationed on a prostrate idol's base,
In vestments of the Vigil of that Feast
The Annunciation, which with annual boon
Whispers, while melting snows dilate those streams
Purer than snows, to universal earth
That Maiden Mother's joy. The Apostle watched

The advancing throng, and gave them welcome thus;
"As though into the great Triumphant Church,
O guests of God, ye flock! Her place is Heaven:
Sirs! we this day are militant below:
Not less, advance in faith. Behold your crowns -
Obedience and Endurance."

There and then
The Rite began: his people's Chief and Head
Beside the font Aengus stood; his face
Sweet as a child's, yet grave as front of eld:
For reverence he had laid his crown aside,
And from the deep hair to the unsandalled feet
Was raimented in white. With mitred head
And massive book, forward Saint Patrick leaned,
Stayed by the gem-wrought crosier. Prayer on prayer
Went up to God; while gift on gift from God,
All Angel-like, invisibly to man,
Descended. Thrice above that princely brow
Patrick the cleansing waters poured, and traced
Three times thereon the Venerable Sign,
Naming the Name Triune. The Rite complete,
Awestruck that concourse downward gazed. At last
Lifting their eyes, they marked the prince's face
That pale it was though bright, anguished and pale,
While from his naked foot a blood-stream gushed
And o'er the pavement welled. The crosier's point,
Weighted with weight of all that priestly form,
Had pierced it through. "Why suffer'dst thou so long
The pain in silence?" Patrick spake, heart-grieved:
Smiling, Aengus answered, "O my Sire,
I thought, thus called to follow Him whose feet
Were pierced with nails, haply the blissful Rite
Bore witness to their sorrows."

At that word
The large eyes of the Apostolic man
Grew larger; and within them lived that light
Not fed by moon or sun, a visible flash
Of that invisible lightning which from God

Vibrates ethereal through the world of souls,
Vivific strength of Saints. The mitred brow
Uptowered sublime: the strong, yet wrinkled hands,
Ascending, ceased not, till the crosier's head
Glittered above the concourse like a star.
At last his hands disparting, down he drew
From Heaven the Royal Blessing, speaking thus:
"For this cause may the blessing, Sire of kings,
Cleave to thy seed forever! Spear and sword
Before them fall! In glory may the race
Of Nafrach's sons, Aengus, and Aileel,
Hold sway on Cashel's summit! Be their kings
Great-hearted men, potent to rule and guard
Their people; just to judge them; warriors strong;
Sage counsellors; faithful shepherds; men of God,
That so through them the everlasting King
May flood their land with blessing." Thus he spake;
And round him all that nation said, "Amen."

Thus held they feast in Cashel of the Kings
That day till all that land was clothed with Christ:
And when the parting came from Cashel's steep
Patrick the People's Blessing thus forth sent:
"The Blessing fall upon the pasture broad,
On fruitful mead, and every corn-clad hill,
And woodland rich with flowers that children love:
Unnumbered be the homesteads, and the hearths: -
A blessing on the women, and the men,
On youth, and maiden, and the suckling babe:
A blessing on the fruit-bestowing tree,
And foodful river tide. Be true; be pure,
Not living from below, but from above,
As men that over-top the world. And raise
Here, on this rock, high place of idols once,
A kingly church to God. The same shall stand
For aye, or, wrecked, from ruin rise restored,
His witness till He cometh. Over Eire
The Blessing speed till time shall be no more
From Cashel of the Kings."

The Saint fared forth:
The People bare him through their kingdom broad
With banner and with song; but o'er its bound
The women of that People followed still
A half day's journey with lamenting voice;
Then silent knelt, lifting their babes on high;
And, crowned with two-fold blessing, home returned.

SAINT PATRICK AND THE CHILDLESS MOTHER

Saint Patrick finds an aged Pagan woman making great lamentation above a tomb which she believes to be that of her son. He kneels beside her in prayer, while around them a wondrous tempest sweeps. After a long time, he declares unto her the Death of Christ, and how, through that Death, the Dead are blessed. Lastly, he dissuades her from her rage of grief, and admonishes her to pray for her son on a tomb hard by, which is his indeed. The woman believes, and, being consoled by a Sign of Heaven, departs in peace.

Across his breast one hundred times each day
Saint Patrick drew the Venerable Sign,
And sixty times by night: and whensoe'er
In travel Cross was seen far off or nigh
On lonely moor, or rock, or heathy hill,
For Erin then was sown with Christian seed,
He sought it, and before it knelt. Yet once,
While cold in winter shone the star of eve
Upon their board, thus spake a youthful monk:
"Three times this day, my father, didst thou pass
The Cross of Christ unmarked. At morn thou saw'st
A last year's lamb that by it sheltered lay,
At noon a dove that near it sat and mourned,
At eve a little child that round it raced,
Well pleased with each; yet saw'st thou not that Cross,
Nor mad'st thou any reverence!" At that word
Wondering, the Saint arose, and left the meat,
And, wondering, went to venerate that Cross.

Dark was the earth and dank ere yet he reached
That spot; and lo! where lamb had lain, and dove
Had mourned, and child had raced, there stood indeed
High-raised, the Cross of Christ. Before it long
He prayed, and kneeling, marked that on a tomb
That Cross was raised. Then, inly moved by God,
The Saint demanded, "Who, of them that walked

The sun-warmed earth lies here in darkness hid?"
And answer made a lamentable Voice:
"Pagan I lived, my own soul's bane: - when dead,
Men buried here my body." Patrick then:
"How stands the Cross of Christ on Pagan grave?"
And answered thus the lamentable Voice:
"A woman's work. She had been absent long;
Her son had died; near mine his grave was made;
Half blind was she through fleeting of her tears,
And, erring, raised the Cross upon my tomb,
Misdeeming it for his. Nightly she comes,
Wailing as only Pagan mothers wail;
So wailed my mother once, while pain tenfold
Ran through my bodiless being. For her sake,
If pity dwells on earth or highest heaven,
May it this mourner comfort! Christian she,
And capable of pity."

Then the Saint
Cried loud, "O God, Thou seest this Pagan's heart,
That love within it dwells: therefore not his
That doom of Souls all hate, and self-exiled
To whom Thy Presence were a woe twice told.
Eternal Pity! pity Thou Thy work; -
Sole Peace of them that love Thee, grant him peace."
Thus Patrick prayed; and in the heaven of heavens
God heard his servant's prayer. Then Patrick mused
"Now know I why I passed that Cross unmarked;
It was not that it seemed."

As thus he knelt,
Behold, upon the cold and bitter wind
Rang wail on wail; and o'er the moor there moved
What seemed a woman's if a human form.
That miserable phantom onward came
With cry succeeding cry that sank or swelled
As dipped or rose the moor. Arrived at last,
She heeded not the Saint, but on that grave
Dashed herself down. Long time that woman wailed;
And Patrick, long, for reverence of her woe

Forbore. At last he spake low-toned as when
Best listener knows not when the strain begins.
"Daughter! the sparrow falls not to the ground
Without his Maker. He that made thy son
Hath sent His Son to bear all woes of men,
And vanquish every foe - the latest, Death."
Then rolled that woman on the Saint an eye
As when the last survivor of a host
Glares on some pitying conqueror. "Ho! the man
That treads upon my grief! He ne'er had sons;
And thou, O son of mine, hast left no sons,
Though oft I said, 'When I am old, his babes
Shall climb my knees.' My boast was mine in youth;
But now mine age is made a barren stock
And as a blighted briar." In grief she turned;
And as on blackening tarn gust follows gust,
Again came wail on wail. On strode the night:
The jagged forehead of that forest old
Alone was seen: all else was gloom. At last
With voice, though kind, upbraiding, Patrick spake:
"Daughter, thy grief is wilful and it errs;
Errs like those sad and tear-bewildered eyes
That for a Christian's take a Pagan's grave,
And for a son's a stranger's. Ah! poor child,
Thy pride it was to raise, where lay thy son,
A Cross, his memory's honour. By thee close
All dewed and glimmering in yon rising moon,
Low lies a grave unhonoured, and unknown:
No cross stands on it; yet upon its breast
Graved shalt thou find what Christian tomb ne'er lacks,
The Cross of Christ. Woman, there lies thy son."

She rose; she found that other tomb; she knelt;
And o'er it went her wandering palms, as though
Some stone-blind mother o'er an infant's face
Should spread an agonising hand, intent
To choose betwixt her own and counterfeit;
She found that cross deep-grav'n, and further sign
Close by, to her well known. One piercing shriek -
Another moment, and her body lay

Along that grave with kisses, and wild hands
As when some forest beast tears up the ground,
Seeking its prey there hidden. Then once more
Rang the wild wail above that lonely heath,
While roared far off the vast invisible woods,
And with them strove the blast, in eddies dire
Whirling both branch and bough. Through hurrying clouds
The scared moon rushed like ship that naked glares
One moment, lightning-lighted in the storm,
Anon in wild waves drowned. An hour went by:
Still wailed that woman, and the tempest roared;
While in the heart of ruin Patrick prayed.
He loved that woman. Unto Patrick dear,
Dear as God's Church was still the single Soul,
Dearest the suffering Soul. He gave her time;
He let the floods of anguish spend themselves:
But when her wail sank low; when woods were mute,
And where the skiey madness late had raged
Shone the blue heaven, he spake with voice in strength
Gentle like that which calmed the Syrian lake,
"My sister, God hath shown me of thy wound,
And wherefore with the blind old Pagan's cry
Hopeless thou mourn'st. Returned from far, thou found'st
Thy son had Christian died, and saw'st the Cross
On Christian graves: and ill thy heart endured
That tomb so dear should lack its reverence meet.
To him thou gav'st the Cross, albeit that Cross
Inly thou know'st not yet. That knowledge thine,
Thou hadst not left thy son amerced of prayer,
And given him tears, not succour." "Yea," she said,
"Of this new Faith I little understand,
Being an aged woman and in woe:
But since my son was Christian, such am I;
And since the Christian tomb is decked with Cross
He shall not lack his right."

Then Patrick spake:
"O woman, hearken, for through me thy son
Invokes thee. All night long for thee, unknown,
My hands have risen: but thou hast raised no prayer

For him, thy dearest; nor from founts of God,
Though brimful, hast thou drawn for lips that thirst.
Arise, and kneel, and hear thy loved one's cry:
Too long he waiteth. Blessed are the dead:
They rest in God's high Will. But more than peace,
The rapturous vision of the Face of God,
Won by the Cross of Christ - for that they thirst
As thou, if viewless stood thy son close by,
Wouldst thirst to see his countenance. Eyes sin-sealed
Not yet can see their God. Prayer speeds the time:
The living help the dead; all praise to Him
Who blends His children in a league of help,
Making all good one good. Eternal Love!
Not thine the will that love should cease with life,
Or, living, cease from service, barren made,
A stagnant gall eating the mourner's heart
That hour when love should stretch a hand of might
Up o'er the grave to heaven. O great in love,
Perfect love's work: for well, sad heart, I know,
Hadst thou not trained thy son in virtuous ways,
Christian he ne'er had been."

Those later words
That solitary mourner understood,
The earlier but in part, and answered thus:
"A loftier Cross, and farther seen, shall rise
Upon this grave new-found! No hireling hands -
Mine own shall raise it; yea, though thirty years
Should sweat beneath the task." And Patrick said:
"What means the Cross? That lore thou lack'st now learn."

Then that which Kings desired to know, and seers
And prophets vigil-blind - that Crown of Truths,
Scandal of fools, yet conqueror of the world,
To her, that midnight mourner, he divulged,
Record authentic: how in sorrow and sin
The earth had groaned; how pity, like a sword,
Had pierced the great Paternal Heart in heaven;
How He, the Light of Light, and God of God,
Had man become, and died upon the Cross,

Vanquishing thus both sorrow and sin, and risen,
The might of death o'erthrown; and how the gates
Of heaven rolled inwards as the Anointed King
Resurgent and ascending through them passed
In triumph with His Holy Dead; and how
The just, thenceforth death-freed, the selfsame gates
Entering, shall share the everlasting throne.
Thus Patrick spake, and many a stately theme
Rehearsed beside, higher than heaven, and yet
Near as the farthest can alone be near.
Then in that grief-worn creature's bosom old
Contentions rose, and fiercer fires than burn
In sultry breasts of youth: and all her past,
Both good and evil, woke, in sleep long sealed;
And all the powers and forces of her soul
Rushed every way through darkness seeking light,
Like winds or tides. Beside her Patrick prayed,
And mightier than his preaching was his prayer,
Sheltering that crisis dread. At last beneath
The great Life-Giver's breath that Human Soul,
An inner world vaster than planet worlds,
In undulation swayed, as when of old
The Spirit of God above the waters moved
Creative, while the blind and shapeless void
Yearned into form, and form grew meet for life,
And downward through the abysses Law ran forth
With touch soul-soft, and seas from lands retired,
And light from dark, and wondering Nature passed
Through storm to calm, and all things found their home.

Silence long time endured; at last, clear-voiced,
Her head not turning, thus the woman spake:
"That God who Man became - who died, and lives, -
Say, died He for my son?" And Patrick said,
"Yea, for thy son He died. Kneel, woman, kneel!
Nor doubt, for mighty is a mother's prayer,
That He who in the eternal light is throned,
Lifting the roseate and the nail-pierced palm,
Will make in heaven the Venerable Sign,
For He it is prays in us, and that Soul

Thou lov'st pass on to glory."

At his word
She knelt, and unto God, with help of God,
Uprushed the strength of prayer, as when the cloud
Uprushes past some beetling mountain wall
From billowy deeps unseen. Long time she prayed;
While heaven and earth grew silent as that night
When rose the Saviour. Sudden ceased the prayer:
And rang upon the night her jubilant cry,
"I saw a Sign in Heaven. Far inward rolled
The gates; and glory flashed from God; and he
I love his entrance won." Then, fair and tall,
That woman stood with hands upraised to heaven
The dusky shadow of her youth renewed,
And instant Patrick spake, "Give thanks to God,
And speed thee home, and sleep; and since thy son
No children left, take to thee orphans twain
And rear them, in his honour, unto Christ;
And yearly, when the death-day of thy son
Returns, his birth-day name it; call thy friends;
Give alms; and range the poor around thy door,
So shall they feast, and pray. Woman, farewell:
All night the dark upon thy face hath lain;
Yet shall we know each other, met in heaven."

Then blithe of foot that Mother crossed the moor;
And when she reached her door a zone of white
Loosening along a cloud that walled the east
Revealed the coming dawn. That dawn ere long
Lay, unawaking, on a face serene,
On tearless lids, and quiet, open palms,
On stormless couch and raiment calm that hid
A breast if faded now, yet happier far
Than when in prime its youthful wave first heaved
Rocking a sleeping Infant.

SAINT PATRICK AT THE FEAST OF KNOCK CAE; OR, THE FOUNDING OF MUNGRET

Saint Patrick, being bidden to a feast, discourses on the way against the pride of the Bards, for whom Fiacc pleads. Derball, a scoffer, requires the Saint to remove a mountain. He kneels down and prays, and Derball avers that the mountain moved. Notwithstanding, Derball believes not, but departs. The Saint declares that he saw not whether the mountain moved. He places Nessan over his convent at Mungret because he had given a little wether to the hungry. Nessan's mother grudged the gift; and Saint Patrick prophesies that her grave shall not be in her son's church.

In Limneach, [1] ere he reached it, fame there ran
Of Patrick's words and works. Before his foot
Aileel had fallen, loud wailing, with his wife,
And cried, "Our child is slain by savage beasts;
But thou, O prophet, if that God thou serv'st
Be God indeed, restore him!" Patrick turned
To Malach, praised of all men. "Brother, kneel,
And raise yon child." But Malach answered, "Nay,
Lest, tempting God, His service I should shame."
Then Patrick, "Answer of the base is thine;
And base shall be that house thou build'st on earth,
Little, and low. A man may fail in prayer:
What then? Thank God! the fault is ours not His,
And ours alone the shame." The Apostle turned
To Ibar, and to Ailbè, bishops twain,
And bade them raise the child. They heard and knelt:
And Patrick knelt between them; and these three
Upheaved a wondrous strength of prayer; and lo!
All pale, yet shining, rose the child, and sat,
Lifting small hands, and preached to those around,
And straightway they believed, and were baptized.

---

[1] Now Limerick.

Thus with loud rumour all the land was full,
And some believed; some doubted; and a chief,
Lonan, the son of Eire, that half believed,
Willing to draw from Patrick wonder and sign,
By messengers besought him, saying, "Come,
For in thy reverence waits thy servant's feast
Spread on Knock Cae." That pleasant hill ascends
Westward of Ara, girt by rivers twain,
Maigue, lily-lighted, and the "Morning Star"
Once "Samhair" named, that eastward through the woods
Winding, upon its rapids earliest meets
The morn, and flings it far o'er mead and plain.

From Limneach therefore Patrick, while the dawn
Still dusk, its joyous secret kept, went forth,
O'er dustless road soon lost in dewy fields,
And groves that, touched by wakening winds, began
To load damp airs with scent. That time it was
When beech leaves lose their silken gloss, and maids
From whitest brows depose the hawthorn white,
Red rose in turn enthroning. Earliest gleams
Glimmered on leaves that shook like wings of birds:
Saint Patrick marked them well. He turned to Fiacc -
"God might have changed to Pentecostal tongues
The leaves of all the forests in the world,
And bade them sing His love! He wrought not thus:
A little hint He gives us and no more.
Alone the willing see. Thus they sin less
Who, if they saw, seeing would disbelieve.
Hark to that note! O foolish woodland choirs!
Ye sing but idle loves; and, idler far,
The bards sing war - war only!"

Answered thus
The monk bard-loving: "Sing it! Ay, and make
The keys of all the tempests hang on zones
Of those cloud-spirits! They, too, can 'bind and loose:'
A bard incensed hath proved a kingdom's doom!
Such Aidan. Upon cakes of meal his host,
King Aileach, fed him in a fireless hall:

The bard complained not - ay, but issuing forth,
Sang in dark wood a keen and venomed song
That raised on the king's countenance plague-spots three;
Who saw him named them Scorn, Dishonour, Shame,
And blighted those three oak trees nigh his door.
What next? Before a month that realm lay drowned
In blood; and fire went o'er the opprobrious house!"
Thus spake the youth, and blushed at his own zeal
For bardic fame; then added, "Strange the power
Of song! My father, do I vainly dream
Oft thinking that the bards, perchance the birds,
Sing something vaster than they think or know?
Some fire immortal lives within their strings:
Therefore the people love them. War divine,
God's war on sin - true love-song best and sweetest -
Perforce they chaunt in spirit, not wars of clans:
Yea, one day, conscious, they shall sing that song;
One day by river clear of south or north,
Pagan no more, the laurelled head shall rise,
And chaunt the Warfare of the Realm of Souls,
The anguish and the cleansing, last the crown -
Prelude of songs celestial!"

Patrick smiled:
"Still, as at first, a lover of the bards!
Hard task was mine to win thee to the cowl!
Dubtach, thy master, sole in Tara's hall
Who made me reverence, mocked my quest. He said,
'Fiacc thou wouldst? - my Fiacc? Few days gone by
I sent the boy with poems to the kings;
He loves me: hardly will he leave the songs
To wear thy tonsure!' As he spake, behold,
Thou enter'dst. Sudden hands on Dubtach's head
I laid, as though to gird with tonsure crown:
Then rose thy clamour, 'Erin's chief of bards
A tonsured man! Me, father, take, not him!
Far less the loss to Erin and the songs!'
Down knelt'st thou; and, ere long, old Dubtach's floor
Shone with thy vernal locks, like forest paths
Made gold by leaves of autumn!"

As he spake,
The sun, new-risen, flashed on a breast of wood
That answered from a thousand jubilant throats:
Then Fiacc, with all their music in his face,
Resumed: "My father, upon Tara's steep
Patient thou sat'st whole months, sifting with care
The laws of Eire, recasting for all time,
Ill laws from good dissevering, as that Day
Shall sever tares from wheat. I see thee still,
As then we saw - thy clenched hand lost in beard
Propping thy chin; thy forehead wrinkle-trenched
Above that wondrous tome, the 'Senchus Mohr,'
Like his, that Hebrew lawgiver's, who sat
Throned on the clouded Mount, while far below
The Tribes waited in awe. Now answer make!
Three bishops, and three brehons, and three kings.
Ye toiled - who helped thee best?" "Dubtach, the bard,"
Patrick replied - "Yea, wise was he, and knew
Man's heart like his own strings." "All bards are wise,"
Shouted the youth, "except when war they wage
On thee, the wisest. In their music bath
They cleanse man's heart, not less, and thus prepare,
Though hating thee, thy way. The bards are wise
For all except themselves. Shall God not save them,
He who would save the worst? Such grace were hard
Unless, death past, their souls to birds might change,
And in the darksomest grove of Paradise
Lament, amerced, their error, yet rejoice
In souls that walked obedient!" "Darksomest grove,"
Patrick made answer; "darksome is their life;
Darksome their pride, their love, their joys, their hopes;
Darksome, though gleams of happier lore they have,
Their light! Seest thou yon forest floor, and o'er it,
The ivy's flash - earth-light? Such light is theirs:
By such can no man walk."

Thus, gay or grave,
Conversed they, while the Brethren paced behind;
Till now the morn crowded each cottage door

With clustered heads. They reached ere long in woods
A hamlet small. Here on the weedy thatch
White fruit-bloom fell: through shadow, there, went round
The swinging mill-wheel tagged with silver fringe;
Here rang the mallet; there was heard remote
The one note of the love-contented bird.
Though warm the sun, in shade the young spring morn
Was edged with winter yet, and icy film
Glazed the deep ruts. The swarthy smith worked hard,
And working sang; the wheelwright toiled close by;
An armourer next to these: through flaming smoke
Glared the fierce hands that on the anvil fell
In thunder down. A sorcerer stood apart
Kneading Death's messenger, that missile ball,
The *Lia Laimbhè*. To his heart he clasped it,
And o'er it muttered spells with flatteries mixed:
"Hail, little daughter mine! 'Twixt hand and heart
I knead thee! From the Red Sea came that sand
Which, blent with viper's poison, makes thy flesh!
Be thou no shadow wandering on the air!
Rush through the battle gloom as red-combed snake
Cleaves the blind waters! On! like Witch's glance,
Or forkèd flash, or shaft of summer pest,
And woe to him that meets thee! Mouth blood-red
My daughter hath: - not healing be her kiss!"
Thus he. In shade he stood, and phrensy-fired;
And yet he marked who watched him. Without word
Him Patrick passed; but spake to all the rest
With voice so kindly reverent, "Is not this,"
Men asked, "the preacher of the 'Tidings Good?'"
"What tidings? Has he found a mine?" "He speaks
To princes as to brothers; to the hind
As we to princes' children! Yea, when mute,
Saith not his face 'Rejoice'?"

At times the Saint
Laid on the head of age his strong right hand,
Gentle as touch of soft-accosting eyes;
And once before an open door he stopped,
Silent. Within, all glowing like a rose,

A mother stood for pleasure of her babes
That - in them still the warmth of couch late left -
Around her gambolled. On his face, as hers,
Their sport regarding, long time lay the smile;
Then crept a shadow o'er it, and he spake
In sadness: "Woman! when a hundred years
Have passed, with opening flower and falling snow,
Where then will be thy children?" Like a cloud
Fear and great wrath fell on her. From the wall
She snatched a battle-axe and raised it high
In both hands, clamouring, "Wouldst thou slay my babes?"
He answered, "I would save them. Woman, hear!
Seest thou yon floating shape? It died a worm;
It lives, the blue-winged angel of spring meads.
Thy children, likewise, if they serve my King,
Death past, shall find them wings." Then to her cheek
The bloom returned, and splendour to her eye;
And catching to her breast, that larger swelled,
A child, she wept, "Oh, would that he might live
For ever! Prophet, speak! thy words are good!
Their father, too, must hear thee." Patrick said,
"Not so; nor falls this seed on every road;"
Then added thus: "You child, by all the rest
Cherished as though he were some infant God,
Is none of thine." She answered, "None of ours;
A great chief sent him here for fosterage."
Then he: "All men on earth the children are
Of One who keeps them here in fosterage:
They see not yet His face; but He sees them,
Yea, and decrees their seasons and their times:
Like infants, they must learn Him first by touch,
Through nature, and her gifts - by hearing next,
The hearing of the ear, and that is Faith -
By Vision last. Woman, these things are hard;
But thou to Limneach come in three days' time,
Likewise thy husband; there, by Sangul's Well,
Thou shalt know all."

The Saint had reached ere long
That festal mount. Thousands with bannered line

Scaled it light-hearted. Never favourite lamb
In ribands decked shone brighter than that hour
The fair flank of Knock Cae. Heath-scented airs
Lightened the clambering toil. At times the Saint
Stayed on their course the crowds, and towards the Truth
Drew them by parable, or record old,
Oftener by question sage. Not all believed:
Of such was Derball. Man of wealth and wit,
Nor wise, nor warlike, toward the Saint he strode
With bubble-seething brain, and head high tossed,
And cried, "Great Seer! remove yon mountain blue,
Cenn Abhrat, by thy prayer! That done, to thee
Fealty I pledge." Saint Patrick knelt in prayer:
Soon Derball cried, "The central ridge descends; -
Southward, beyond it, Longa's lake shines out
In sunlight flashing!" At his word drew near
The men of Erin. Derball homeward turned,
Mocking: "Believe who will, believe not I!
Me more imports it o'er my foodful fields
To draw the Maigue's rich waters than to stare
At moving hills." But certain of that throng,
Light men, obsequious unto Derball's laugh,
Questioned of Patrick if the mountain moved.
He answered, "On the ground mine eyes were fixed;
Nought saw I. Haply, through defect of mine,
It moved not. Derball said the mountain moved;
Yet kept he not his pledge, but disbelieved.
'Faith can move mountains.' Never said my King
That mountains moved could move reluctant faith
In unbelieving heart." With sad, calm voice
He spake; and Derball's laughter frustrate died.

Meantime, high up on that thyme-scented hill
By shadows swept, and lights, and rapturous winds,
Lonan prepared the feast, and, with that chief,
Mantan, a deacon. Tables fair were spread;
And tents with branches gay. Beside those tents
Stood the sweet-breathing, mournful, slow-eyed kine
With hazel-shielded horns, and gave their milk
Gravely to merry maidens. Low the sun

Had fallen, when, Patrick near the summit now,
There burst on him a wandering troop, wild-eyed,
With scant and quaint array. O'er sunburnt brows
They wore sere wreaths; their piebald vests were stained,
And lean their looks, and sad: some piped, some sang,
Some tossed the juggler's ball. "From far we came,"
They cried; "we faint with hunger; give as food!"
Upon them Patrick bent a pitying eye,
And said, "Where Lonan and where Mantan toil
Go ye, and pray them, for mine honour's sake,
To gladden you with meat." But Lonan said,
And Mantan, "Nay, but when the feast is o'er,
The fragments shall be yours." With darkening brow
The Saint of that denial heard, and cried,
"He cometh from the North, even now he cometh,
For whom the Blessing is reserved; he cometh
Bearing a little wether at his back:"
And, straightway, through the thicket evening-dazed
A shepherd - by him walked his mother - pushed,
Bearing a little wether. Patrick said,
"Give them to eat. They hunger." Gladly then
That shepherd youth gave them the wether small:
With both his hands outstretched, and liberal smile,
He gave it, though, with angry eye askance
His mother grudged it sore. The wether theirs,
As though earth-swallowed, vanished that wild tribe,
Fearing that mother's eye.

Then Patrick spake
To Lonan, "Zealous is thy service, friend;
Yet of thy house no king shall sit on throne,
No bishop bless the people." Turning then
To Mantan, thus he spake, "Careful art thou
Of many things; not less that church thou raisest
Shall not be of the honoured in the land;
And in its chancel waste the mountain kine
Shall couch above thy grave." To Nessan last
Thus spake he: "Thou that didst the hungry feed,
The poor of Christ, that know not yet His name,
And, helping them that cried to me for help,

Cherish mine honour, like a palm, one day,
Shall rise thy greatness." Nessan's mother old
For pardon knelt. He blessed her hoary head,
Yet added, mournful, "Not within the Church
That Nessan serves shall lie his mother's grave."
Then Nessan he baptized, and on him bound
Ere long the deacon's grade, and placed him, later,
Priest o'er his church at Mungret. Centuries ten
It stood, a convent round it as a star
Forth sending beams of glory and of grace
O'er woods Teutonic and the Tyrrhene Sea.
Yet Nessan's mother in her son's great church
Slept not; nor where the mass bell tinkled low:
West of the church her grave, to his - her son's -
Neighbouring, yet severed by the chancel wall.

Thus from the morning star to evening star
Went by that day. In Erin many such
Saint Patrick lived, using well pleased the chance,
Or great or small, since all things come from God:
And well the people loved him, being one
Who sat amid their marriage feasts, and saw,
Where sin was not, in all things beauty and love.
But, ere he passed from Munster, longing fell
On Patrick's heart to view in all its breadth
Her river-flood, and bless its western waves;
Therefore, forth journeying, to that hill he went,
Highest among the wave-girt, heathy hills,
That still sustains his name, and saw the flood
At widest stretched, and that green Isle [1] hard by,
And northern Thomond. From its coasts her sons
Rushed countless forth in skiff and coracle
Smiting blue wave to white, till Sheenan's sound
Ceased, in their clamour lost. That hour from God
Power fell on Patrick; and in spirit he saw,
Invisible to flesh, the western coasts,
And the ocean way, and, far beyond, that land
The Future's heritage, and prophesied

---

[1] Foynes.

Of Brendan who ere long in wicker boat
Should over-ride the mountains of the deep,
Shielded by God, and tread - no fable then -
Fabled Hesperia. Last of all he saw
More near, thy hermit home, Senanus; - 'Hail,
Isle of blue ocean and the river's mouth!
The People's Lamp, their Counsel's Head, is thine!"
That hour shone out through cloud the westering sun
And paved the wave with fire: that hour not less
Strong in his God, westward his face he set,
Westward and north, and spread his arms abroad,
And drew the blessing down, and flung it far:
"A blessing on the warriors, and the clans,
A blessing on high field, and golden vales,
On sea-like plain and on the showery ridge,
On river-ripple, cliff, and murmuring deep,
On seaward peaks, harbours, and towns, and ports;
A blessing on the sand beneath the ships:
On all descend the Blessing!" Thus he prayed,
Great-hearted; and from all the populous hills
And waters came the People's vast "Amen!"

SAINT PATRICK AND KING EOCHAID

King Eochaid submits himself to the Christian Law because Saint Patrick has delivered his son from bonds, yet only after making a pact that he is not, like the meaner sort, to be baptized. In this stubbornness he persists, though otherwise a kindly king; and after many years, he dies. Saint Patrick had refused to see his living face; yet after death he prays by the death-bed. Life returns to the dead; and sitting up, like one sore amazed, he demands baptism. The Saint baptizes him, and offers him a choice either to reign over all Erin for fifteen years, or to die. Eochaid chooses to die, and so departs.

Eochaid, son of Crimther, reigned, a King
Northward in Clochar. Dearer to his heart
Than kingdom or than people or than life
Was he, the boy long wished for. Dear was she,
Keinè, his daughter. Babyhood's white star,
Beauteous in childhood, now in maiden dawn
She witched the world with beauty. From her eyes
A light went forth like morning o'er the sea;
Sweeter her voice than wind on harp; her smile
Could stay men's breath. With wingèd feet she trod
The yearning earth that, if it could, like waves
Had swelled to meet their pressure. Ah, the pang!
Beauty, the immortal promise, like a cheat
If unwed glides into the shadow land,
Childless and twice defeated. Beauty wed
To mate unworthy, suffers worse eclipse -
"Ill choice between two ills!" thus spleenfull cried
Eochaid; but not his the pensive grief:
He would have kept his daughter in his house
For ever; yet, since better might not be,
Himself he chose her out a mate, and frowned,
And said, "The dog must have her." But the maid
Wished not for marriage. Tender was her heart;
Yet though her twentieth year had o'er her flown,
And though her tears had dewed a mother's grave,

In her there lurked, not flower of womanhood,
But flower of angel texture. All around
To her was love. The crown of earthly love
Seemed but its crown of mockery. Love Divine -
For that she yearned, and yet she knew it not;
Knew less that love she feared.

She walked in woods
While all the green leaves, drenched by sunset's gold,
Upon a shower-bespangled sycamore
Shivered, and birds among them choir on choir
Chanted her praise - or spring's. "Ill sung," she laughed,
"My dainty minstrels! Grant to me your wings,
And I for them will teach you song of mine:
Listen!" A carol from her lip there gushed
That, ere its time, might well have called the spring
From winter's coldest cave. It ceased; she turned.
Beside her Patrick stood. His hand he raised
To bless her. Awed, though glad, upon her knees
The maiden sank. His eye, as if through air,
Saw through that stainless soul, and, crystal-shrined
Therein, its inmate, Truth. That other Truth
Instant to her he preached - the Truth Divine -
(For whence is caution needful, save from sin?)
And those two Truths, each gazing upon each,
Embraced like sisters, thenceforth one. For her
No arduous thing was Faith, ere yet she heard
In heart believing: and, as when a babe
Marks some bright shape, if near or far, it knows not,
And stretches forth a witless hand to clasp
Phantom or form, even so with wild surmise
And guesses erring first, and questions apt,
She chased the flying light, and round it closed
At last, and found it substance. "This is He."
Then cried she, "This, whom every maid should love,
Conqueror self-sacrificed of sin and death:
How shall we find, how please Him, how be nigh?"
Patrick made answer: "They that do His will
Are nigh Him." And the virgin: "Of the nigh,
Say, who is nighest?" Thus, that wingèd heart

Rushed to its rest. He answered: "Nighest they
Who offer most to Him in sacrifice,
As when the wedded leaves her father's house
And cleaveth to her husband. Nighest they
Who neither father's house nor husband's house
Desire, but live with Him in endless prayer,
And tend Him in His poor." Aloud she cried,
"The nearest to the Highest, that is love; -
I choose that bridal lot!" He answered, "Child,
The choice is God's. For each, that lot is best
To which He calls us." Lifting then pure hands,
Thus wept the maiden: "Call me, Virgin-born!
Will not the Mother-Maid permit a maid
To sit beside those nail-pierced feet, and wipe,
With hair untouched by wreaths of mortal love,
The dolorous blood-stains from them? Stranger guest,
Come to my father's tower! Against my will,
Against his own, in bridal bonds he binds me:
My suit he might resist: he cannot thine!"

She spake; and by her Patrick paced with feet
To hers accordant. Soon they reached that fort:
Central within a circling rath earth-built
It stood; the western tower of stone; the rest,
Not high, but spreading wide, of wood compact;
For thither many a forest hill had sent
His wind-swept daughter brood, relinquishing
Converse with cloud and beam and rain forever
To echo back the revels of a Prince.
Mosaic was the work, beam laced with beam
In quaint device: high up, o'er many a door
Shone blazon rich of vermeil, or of green,
Or shield of bronze, glittering with veinèd boss,
Chalcedony or agate, or whate'er
The wave-lipped marge of Neagh's broad lake might boast,
Or ocean's shore, northward from Brandon's Head
To where the myriad-pillared cliffs hang forth
Their stony organs o'er the lonely main.
And trembles yet the pilgrim, noting at eve

The pride Fomorian, and that Giant Way [1]
Trending toward eastern Alba. From his throne
Above the semicirque of grassy seats
Whereon by Brehons and by Ollambs girt
Daily be judged his people, rose the king
And bade the stranger welcome.

Day to day
And night to night succeeded. In fit time,
For Patrick, sometimes sudden, oft was slow,
He spoke his Master's message. At the close,
As though in trance, the warriors circling stood
With hands outstretched; the Druids downward frowned,
Silent; and like a strong man awed for once,
Eochaid round him stared. A little while,
And from him passed the amazement. Buoyant once more,
And bright like trees fresher for thunder-shower,
With all his wonted aspect, bold and keen,
He answered: "O my prophet, words, words, words!
We too have Prophets. Better thrice our Bards;
Yet, being no better these than trumpet's blast,
The trumpet more I prize. Had words been work,
Myself in youth had led the loud-voiced clan!
Deeds I preferred. What profit e'er had I
From windy marvels? Once with me in war
A seer there camped that, bending back his head,
Fit rites performed, and upward gazing, blew
With rounded lips into the heaven of heavens
Druidic breath. That heaven was changed to cloud,
Cloud that on borne to Clairè's hated bound
Down fell, a rain of blood! To me what gain?
Within three weeks my son was trapped and snared
By Aodh of Hy Brinin, king whose hosts
Number my warriors fourfold. Three long years
Beyond those purple mountains in the west
Hostage he lies." Lightly Eochaid spake,
And turned: but shaken chin betrayed that grief
Which lived beneath his lightness.

---

[1] The Giant's Causeway.

Sudden thronged
High on the neighbouring hills a jubilant troop,
Their banners waving, while the midway vale
With harp and horn resounded. Patrick spake:
"Rejoice! thy son returns! not sole he comes,
But in his hand a princess, fair and good,
A kingdom for her dowry. Aodh's realm,
By me late left, welcomed *my* King with joy:
All fire the mountains shone. 'The God I serve,'
Thus spake I, Aodh pointing to those fires,
'In mountains of rejoicing hath no joy
While sad beyond them sits a childless man,
His only son thy captive. Captive groaned
Creation; Bethlehem's Babe set free the slave.
For His sake loose thy thrall!' A sweeter voice
Pleaded with mine, his daughter's 'mid her tears.
'Aodh,' I said, 'these two each other love!
What think'st thou? He who shaped the linnet's nest,
Indifferent unto Him are human loves?
Arise! thy work make perfect! Righteous deeds
Are easier whole than half.' In thought awhile
Old Aodh sat; then to his daughter turned,
And thus, imperious even in kindness, spake:
'Well fought the youth ere captured, like the son
Of kings, and worthy to be sire of kings:
Wed him this hour: and in three days, at eve,
Restore him to his father!' King, this hour
Thou know'st if Christ's strong Faith be empty words,
Or truth, and armed with power."

That night was passed
In feasting and in revel, high and low
Rich with a common gladness. Many a torch
Flared in the hand of servitors hill-sent,
That standing, each behind a guest, retained
Beneath that roof clouded by banquet steam
Their mountain wildness. Here, the splendour glanced
On goblet jewel-chased and dark with wine,
Swift circling; there, on walls with antlers spread,

And rich with yew-wood carvings, flower or bud,
Or clustered grape pendent in russet gleam
As though from nature's hand. A hall hard by
Echoed the harp that now nor kindled rage,
Nor grief condoled, nor sealed with slumber's balm
Tempestuous spirits, triumphs three of song,
But raised to rapture, mirth. Far shone that hall
Glowing with hangings steeped in every tinct
The boast of Erin's dyeing-vats, now plain,
Now pranked with bird or beast or fish, whate'er
Fast-flying shuttle from the craftsman's thought
Catching, on bore through glimmering warp and woof,
A marvellous work; now traced by broiderer's hand
With legends of Ferdìadh and of Meave,
Even to the golden fringe. The warriors paced
Exulting. Oft they showed their merit's prize,
Poniard or cup, tribute ordained of tribes
From age to age, Eochaid's right, on them
With equal right devolving. Slow they moved
In mantle now of crimson, now of blue,
Clasped with huge torque of silver or of gold
Just where across the snowy shirt there strayed
Tendril of purple thread. With jewelled fronts
Beauteous in pride 'mid light of winsome smiles,
Over the rushes green with slender foot
In silver slipper hid, the ladies passed,
Answering with eyes not lips the whispered praise,
Or loud the bride extolling - "When was seen
Such sweetness and such grace?"

Meantime the king
Conversed with Patrick. Vexed he heard announced
His daughter's high resolve: but still his looks
Went wandering to his son. "My boy! Behold him!
His valour and his gifts are all from me:
My first-born!" From the dancing throng apart
His daughter stood the while, serene and pale,
Down-gazing on that lily in her hand
With face of one who notes not shapes around,
But dreams some happy dream. The king drew nigh,

And on her golden head the sceptre staff
Leaning, but not to hurt her, thus began:
"Your prophets of the day, I trust them not!
If sent from God, why came they not long since?
Our Druids came before them, and, belike,
Shall after them abide! With these new seers
I count not Patrick. Things that Patrick says
I ofttimes thought. His lineage too is old -
Wide-browed, grey-eyed, with downward lessening face,
Not like your baser breeds, with questing eyes
And jaw of dog. But for thy Heavenly Spouse,
I like not Him! At least, wed Cormac first!
If rude his ways, yet noble is his name,
And being but poor the man will bide with me:
He's brave, and likeliest soon in fight may fall!
When Cormac dies, wed next - " a music clash
Forth bursting drowned his words.

Three days passed by:
To Patrick, then preparing to depart,
Thus spake Eochaid in the ears of all:
"Herald Heaven-missioned of the Tidings Good!
Those tidings I have pondered. They are true:
I for that truth's sake, and in honour bound
By reason of my son set free, resolve
The same, upon conditions, to believe,
And suffer all my people to believe,
Just terms exacted. Briefly these they are:
First, after death, I claim admittance frank
Into thy Heavenly Kingdom: next, till death
For me exemption from that Baptism Rite,
Imposed on kerne and hind. Experience-taught,
I love not rigid bond and written pledge:
'Tis well to brand your mark on sheep or lamb:
Kings are of lion breed; and of my house
'Tis known there never yet was king baptized.
This pact concluded, preach within my realm
Thy Faith; and wed my daughter to thy God.
Not scholarly am I to know what joy
A maid can find in psalm, and cell, and spouse

Unseen: yet ever thus my sentence stood,
'Choose each his way.' My son restored, her loss
To me is loss the less." Thus spake the king.

Then Patrick, on whose face the princess bent
The supplication softly strong of eyes
Like planets seen through mist, Eochaid's heart
Knowing, which miracle had hardened more,
Made answer, "King, a man of jests art thou,
Claiming free range in heaven, and yet its gate
Thyself close barring! In thy daughter's prayers
Belike thou trustest, that where others creep
Thou shalt its golden bastions over-fly.
Far otherwise than in that way thou ween'st,
That daughter's prayers shall speed thee. With thy word
I close, that word to frustrate. God be with thee!
Thou living, I return not. Fare thee well."
Thus speaking, by the hand he took the maid,

And led her through the concourse. At her feet
The poor fell low, kissing her garment's hem,
And many brought their gifts, and all their prayers,
And old men wept. A maiden train snow-garbed,
Her steps attending, whitened plain and field,
As when at times dark glebe, new-turned, is changed
To white by flock of ocean birds alit,
Or inland blown by storm, or hunger-urged
To filch the late-sown grain. Her convent home
Ere long received her. There Ethembria ruled,
Green Erin's earliest nun. Of princely race,
She in past years before the font of Christ
Had knelt at Patrick's feet. Once more she sought him:
Over the lovely, lovelier change had passed,
As when on childish girlhood, 'mid a shower
Of lilies earthward wafted, maidenhood
In peacefuller state assumes her spotless throne;
So, from that maiden, vestal now had risen: -
Lowlier she seemed, more tender, soft, and grave,
Yet loftier; hushed in quiet more divine,
Yet wonder-awed. Again she knelt, and o'er

The bending queenly head, till then unbent,
He flung that veil which woman bars from man
To make her more than woman. Nigh to death
The Saint forgat not her. With her remained
Keinè; but Patrick dwelt far off at Saul.

Years came and went: yet neither chance nor change,
Nor war, nor peace, nor warnings from the priests,
Nor whispers 'mid the omen-mongering crowd,
Might from Eochaid charm his wayward will,
Nor reasonings of the wise that still preferred
Safe port to victory's pride. He reasoned too,
For confident in his reasonings was the king,
Reckoning on pointed fingers every link
That clenched his mail of proof. "On Patrick's word
Ye tell me Baptism is the gate of Heaven:
Attend, Sirs! I have Patrick's word no less
That I shall enter Heaven. What need I more?
If, Death, truth-speaker, shows that Patrick lied,
Plain is my right against him! Heaven not won,
Patrick bare hence my daughter through a fraud:
He must restore her fourfold - daughters four,
As fair and good. If not, the prophet's pledge
For honour's sake his Master must redeem,
And unbaptized receive me. Dupes are ye!
Doomed 'mid the common flock, with branded fleece
Bleating to enter Heaven!"

The years went by;
And weakness came. No more his small light form
To reverent eyes seemed taller than it was:
No more the shepherd watched him from the hill
Heading his hounds, and hoped to catch his smile,
Yet feared his questions keen. The end drew near.
Some wept, some railed; restless the warriors tramped;
The Druids conned their late discountenanced spells;
The bard his lying harpstrings spurned, so long
Healing, unhelpful now. But far away,
Within that lonely convent tower from her
Who prayed for ever, mightier rose the prayer.

Within the palace, now by usage old
To all flung open, all were sore amazed,
All save the king. The leech beside the bed
Sobbed where he stood, yet sware, "The fit will pass:
Ten years the King may live." Eochaid frowned:
"Shall I, to patch thy fame, live ten years more,
My death-time come? My seventy years are sped:
My sire and grandsire died at sixty-nine.
Like Aodh, shall I lengthen out my days
Toothless, nor fit to vindicate my clan,
Some losel's song? The kingdom is my son's!
Strike from my little milk-white horse the shoes,
And loose him where the freshets make the mead
Greenest in springtide. He must die ere long;
And not to him did Patrick open Heaven.
Praise be to Patrick's God! May He my sins,
Known and unknown, forgive!"

Backward he sank
Upon his bed, and lay with eyes half closed,
Murmuring at times one prayer, five words or six;
And twice or thrice he spake of trivial things;
Then like an infant slumbered till the sun,
Sinking beneath a great cloud's fiery skirt,
Smote his old eyelids. Waking, in his ears
The ripening cornfields whispered 'neath the breeze,
For wide were all the casements that the soul
By death delivered hindrance none might find
(Careful of this the king); and thus he spake:
"Nought ever raised my heart to God like fields
Of harvest, waving wide from hill to hill,
All bread-full for my people. Hale me forth:
When I have looked once more upon that sight
My blessing I will give them, and depart."

Then in the fields they laid him, and he spake.
"May He that to my people sends the bread,
Send grace to all who eat it!" With that word
His hands down-falling, back once more he sank,

And lay as dead; yet, sudden, rising not,
Nor moving, nor his eyes unclosing, said,
"My body in the tomb of ancient kings
Inter not till beside it Patrick stands
And looks upon my brow." He spake, then sighed
A little sigh, and died.

Three days, as when
Black thunder cloud clings fast to mountain brows,
So to the nation clung the grief: three days
The lamentation sounded on the hills
And rang around the pale blue meres, and rose
Shrill from the bleeding heart of vale and glen,
And rocky isle, and ocean's moaning shore;
While by the bier the yellow tapers stood,
And on the right side knelt Eochaid's son,
Behind him all the chieftains cloaked in black;
And on his left his daughter knelt, the nun,
Behind her all her sisterhood, white-veiled,
Like tombstones after snowstorm. Far away,
At "Saul of Patrick," dwelt the Saint when first
The king had sickened. Message sent he none
Though knowing all; and when the end was nigh,
And heralds now besought him day by day,
He made no answer till o'er eastern seas
Advanced the third fair morning. Then he rose,
And took the Staff of Jesus, and at eve
Beside the dead king standing, on his brow
Fixed a sad eye. Aloud the people wept;
The kneeling warriors eyed their lord askance;
The nuns intoned their hymn. Above that hymn
A cry rang out: it was the daughter's prayer;
And after that was silence. By the dead
Still stood the Saint, nor e'er removed his gaze.
Then - seen of all - behold, the dead king's hands
Rose slowly, as the weed on wave upheaved
Without its will; and all the strengthless shape
In cerements wrapped, as though by mastering voice
From the white void evoked and realm of death,
Without its will, a gradual bulk half rose,

The hoar head gazing forth. Upon the face
Had passed a change, the greatest earth may know;
For what the majesty of death began
The majesties of worlds unseen, and life
Resurgent ere its time, had perfected,
All accidents of flesh and sorrowful years
Cancelled and quelled. Yet horror from his eyes
Looked out as though some vision once endured
Must cling to them for ever. Patrick spake:
"Soul from the dead sent back once more to earth
What seek'st thou from God's Church?" He answer made,
"Baptism." Then Patrick o'er him poured the might
Of healing waters in the Name Triune,
The Father, and the Son, and Holy Spirit;
And from his eyes the horror passed, and light
Went from them, as the light of eyes that rest
On the everlasting glory, while he spake:
"Tempest of darkness drave me past the gates
Celestial, and, a moment's space, within
I heard the hymning of the hosts of God
That feed for ever on the Bread of Life
As feed the nations on the harvest wheat.
Tempest of darkness drave me to the gates
Of Anguish: then a cry came up from earth,
Cry like my daughter's when her mother died,
That stayed the on-rushing whirlwind; yet mine eyes
Perforce looked in, and, many a thousand years,
Branded upon them lay that woful sight
Now washed from them for ever." Patrick spake:
"This day a twofold choice I give thee, son;
For fifteen years the rule o'er Erin's land,
Rule absolute, Ard-Righ o'er lesser kings;
Or instant else to die, and hear once more
That hymn celestial, and that Vision see
They see who sing that anthem." Light from God
Over that late dead countenance streamed amain,
Like to his daughter's now - more beauteous thrice -
Yet awful, more than beauteous. "Rule o'er earth,
Rule without end, were nought to that great hymn
Heard but a single moment. I would die."

Then Patrick, on him gazing, answered, "Die!"
And died the king once more, and no man wept;
But on her childless breast the nun sustained
Softly her father's head.

That night discourse
Through hall and court circled in whispers low.
First one, "Was that indeed our king? But where
The sword-scar and the wrinkles?" "Where," rejoined,
Wide-eyed, the next, "his little cranks and girds
The wisdom, and the whim?" Then Patrick spake:
"Sirs, till this day ye never saw your king;
The man ye doted on was but his mask,
His picture - yea, his phantom. Ye have seen
At last the man himself." That night nigh sped,
While slowly o'er the darkling woods went down,
Warned by the cold breath of the up-creeping morn
Invisible yet nigh, the August moon,
Two vestals, gliding past like moonlight gleams,
Conversed: one said, "His daughter's prayer prevailed!"
The second, "Who may know the ways of God?
For this, may many a heart one day rejoice
In hope! For this, the gift to many a man
Exceed the promise; Faith's invisible germ
Quickened with parting breath; and Baptism given,
It may be, by an angel's hand unseen!"

SAINT PATRICK AND THE FOUNDING OF ARMAGH CATHEDRAL

Saint Patrick repairs to Ardmacha, there to found the chief church of Erin. For that purpose he demands of Dairè, the king, a certain woody hill. The king refuses it, and afterwards treats him with alternate scorn and reverence; while the Saint, in each event alike, makes the same answer, "Deo Gratias." At last the king concedes to him the hill; and on the summit of it Saint Patrick finds a little white fawn asleep. The men of Erin would have slain that fawn; but the Saint carries it on his shoulder, and restores it to its dam. Where the fawn lay, he places the altar of his cathedral.

At Cluain Cain, in Ross, unbent yet old,
Dwelt Patrick long. Its sweet and flowery sward
He to the rock had delved, with fixed resolve
To build thereon Christ's chiefest church in Eire.
Then by him stood God's angel, speaking thus:
"Not here, but northward." He replied, "O, would
This spot might favour find with God! Behold!
Fair is it, and as meet to clasp a church
As is a true heart in a virgin breast
To clasp the Faith of Christ. The hinds around
Name it 'the beauteous meadow.'" "Fair it is,"
The angel answered, "nor shall lack its crown.
Another's is its beauty. Here, one day
A pilgrim from the Britons sent shall build,
And, later, what he builds shall pass to thine;
But thou to Macha get thee."

Patrick then,
Obedient as that Patriarch Sire who faced
At God's command the desert, northward went
In holy silence. Soon to him was lost
That green and purple meadow-sea, embayed
'Twixt two descending woody promontories,
Its outlet girt with isles of rock, its shores

Cream-white with meadow-sweet. Not once he turned,
Climbing the uplands rough, or crossing streams
Swoll'n by the melted snows. The Brethren paced
Behind; Benignus first, his psalmist; next
Secknall, his bishop; next his brehon Erc;
Mochta, his priest; and Sinell of the Bells;
Rodan, his shepherd; Essa, Bite, and Tassach,
Workers of might in iron and in stone,
God-taught to build the churches of the Faith
With wisdom and with heart-delighting craft;
Mac Cairthen last, the giant meek that oft
On shoulders broad bare Patrick through the floods:
His rest was nigh. That hour they crossed a stream;
'Twas deep, and, 'neath his load, the giant sighed.
Saint Patrick said, "Thou wert not wont to sigh!"
He answered, "Old I grow. Of them my mates
How many hast thou left in churches housed
Wherein they rule and rest!" The Saint replied,
"Thee also will I leave within a church
For rule and rest; not to mine own too near
For rarely then should we be seen apart,
Nor yet remote, lest we should meet no more."
At Clochar soon he placed him. There, long years
Mac Cairthen sat, its bishop.

As they went,
Oft through the woodlands rang the battle-shout;
And twice there rose above the distant hill
The smoke of hamlet fired. Yet, none the less,
Spring-touched, the blackbird sang; the cowslip changed
Green lawn to green and golden; and grey rock
And river's marge with primroses were starred;
Here shook the windflower; there the blue-bells gleamed,
As though a patch of sky had fallen on earth.

Then to Benignus spake the Saint: "My son,
If grief were lawful in a world redeemed
The blood-stains on a land so strong in faith,
So slack in love, might cloud the holiest brow,
Yea, his whose head lay on the breast of Christ.

Clan wars with clan: no injury is forgiven;
Like to the joy in stag-hunts is the war:
Alas! for such what hope!" Benignus answered
"O Father, cease not for this race to hope,
Lest they should hope no longer! Hope they have;
Still say they, 'God will snare us in the end
Though wild.'" And Patrick, "Spirits twain are theirs:
The stranger, and the poor, at every door
They meet, and bid him in. The youngest child
Officious is in service; maids prepare
The bath; men brim the wine-cup. Then, forth borne,
Cities they fire and rich in spoil depart,
Greed mixed with rage - an industry of blood!"
He spake, and thus the younger made reply:
"Father, the stranger is the brother-man
To them; the poor is neighbour. Septs remote
To them are alien worlds. They know not yet
That rival clans are men."

"That know they shall,"
Patrick made answer, "when a race far off
Tramples their race to clay! God sends abroad
His plague of war that men on earth may know
Brother from foe, and anguish work remorse."
He spake, and after musings added thus:
"Base of God's kingdom is Humility -
I have not spared to thunder o'er their pride;
Great kings have I rebuked and signs sent forth,
And banned for their sake fruitful plain, and bay;
Yet still the widow's cry is on the air,
The orphan's wail!" Benignus answered mild,
"O Father, not alone with sign and ban
Hast thou rebuked their madness. Oftener far
Thy sweetness hath reproved them. Once in woods
Northward of Tara as we tracked our way
Round us there gathered slaves who felled the pines
For ship-masts. Scarred their hands, and red with blood,
Because their master, Trian, thus had sworn,
'Let no man sharpen axe!' Upon those hands
Gazing, they wept soon as thy voice they heard,

Because that voice was soft. Thou heard'st their tale;
Straight to that chieftain's castle went'st thou up,
And bound'st him with thy fast, beside his gate
Sitting in silence till his heart should melt;
And since he willed it not to melt, he died.
Then, in her arms two babes, came forth the queen
Black-robed, and freed her slaves, and gave them hire;
And, we returning after many years,
Filled was that wood with homesteads; plots of corn
Rustled around them; here were orchards; there
In trench or tank they steeped the bright blue flax;
The saw-mill turned to use the wanton brook;
Murmured the bee-hive; murmured household wheel;
Soft eyes looked o'er it through the dusk; at work
The labourers carolled; matrons glad and maids
Bare us the pail head-steadied, children flowers:
Last, from her castle paced the queen, and led
In either hand her sons whom thou hadst blest,
Thenceforth to stand thy priests. The land believed;
And not through ban, or word, sharp-edged or soft,
But silence and thy fast the ill custom died."

He answered, "Christ, in Christ-like life expressed,
This, this, not words, subdues a land to Christ;
And in this best Apostolate all have part.
Ah me! that flower thou hold'st is strong to preach
Creative Love, because itself is lovely;
But we, the heralds of Redeeming Love,
Because we are unlovely in our lives,
Preach to deaf ears! Yet theirs, theirs too, the sin."
Benignus made reply: "The race is old;
Not less their hearts are young. Have patience with them!
For see, in spring the grave old oaks push forth
Impatient sprays, wine-red: their strength matured,
These sober down to verdure." Patrick paused,
Then, brooding, spake, as one who thinks, not speaks:
"A priest there walked with me ten years and more;
Warrior in youth was he. One day we heard
The shock of warring clans - I hear it still:
Within him, as in darkening vase you note

The ascending wine, I watched the passion mount: -
Sudden he dashed him down into the fight,
Nor e'er to Christ returned." Benignus answered;
"I saw above a dusky forest roof
The glad spring run, leaving a track sea-green:
Not straight she ran; and yet she reached her goal:
Later I saw above green copse of thorn
The glad spring run, leaving a track foam-white:
Not straight she ran; yet soon she conquered all!
O Father, is it sinful to be glad
Here amid sin and sorrow? Joy is strong,
Strongest in spring-tide! Mourners I have known
That, homeward wending from the new-dug grave,
Against their will, where sang the happy birds
Have felt the aggressive gladness stir their hearts,
And smiled amid their tears." So babbled he,
Shamed at his spring-tide raptures.

As they went,
Far on their left there stretched a mighty land
Of forest-girdled hills, mother of streams:
Beyond it sank the day; while round the west
Like giants thronged the great cloud-phantoms towered.
Advancing, din they heard, and found in woods
A hamlet and a field by war unscathed,
And boys on all sides running. Placid sat
The village Elders; neither lacked that hour
The harp that gently tranquillises age,
Yet wakes young hearts with musical unrest,
Forerunner oft of love's unrest. Ere long
The measure changed to livelier: maid with maid
Danced 'mid the dancing shadows of the trees,
And youth with youth; till now, the strangers near,
Those Elders welcomed them with act benign;
And soon was slain the fatted kid, and soon
The lamb; nor any asked till hunger's rage
Was quelled, "Who art thou?" Patrick made reply,
"A Priest of God." Then prayed they, "Offer thou
To Him our sacrifice! Belike 'tis He
Who saves from war this hamlet hid in woods:

Unblest be he who finds it!" Thus they spake,
The matrons, not the youths. In friendly talk
The hours went by with laughter winged and tale;
But when the moon, on rolling through the heavens,
Showered through the leaves a dew of sprinkled light
O'er the dark ground, the maidens garments brought
Woven in their quiet homes when nights were long,
Red cloak and kirtle green, and laid them soft,
Still with the wearers' blameless beauty warm,
For coverlet upon the warm dry grass,
Honouring the stranger guests. For these they deemed
Their low-roofed cots too mean. Glad-hearted rose
The Christian hymn, not timid: far it rang
Above the woods. Ere long, their blissful rites
Fulfilled, the wanderers laid them down and slept.

At midnight by the side of Patrick stood
Victor, God's Angel, saying, "Lo! thy work
Hath favour found and thou ere long shalt die:
Thus therefore saith the Lord, 'So long as sea
Girdeth this isle, so long thy name shall hang
In splendour o'er it, like the stars of God.'"
Then Patrick said, "A boon! I crave a boon!"
The angel answered, "Speak;" and Patrick said,
"Let them that with me toiled, or in the years
To come shall toil, building o'er all this land
The Fortress-Temple and great House of Christ,
Equalled with me my name in Erin share."
And Victor answered, "Half thy prayer is thine;
With thee shall they partake. Not less, thy name
Higher than theirs shall rise, and wider spread,
Since thus more plainly shall His glory shine
Whose glory is His justice."

With the morn
Those pilgrims rose, and, prime entoned and lauds,
Poured out their blessing on that woodland clan
Which, round them pressing, kissed them, robe and knee;
Then on they journeyed till at set of sun
Shone out the roofs of Macha, and that tower

Where Dairè dwelt, its lord.

Saint Patrick sent
To Dairè embassage, vouchsafing prayer
As sire might pray of son; "Give thou yon hill
To Christ, that we may build His church thereon."
And Dairè answered with a brow of storms
Bent forward darkly, and long, sneering lips,
"Your master is a mighty man, we know.
Garban, that lied to God, he slew through prayer,
And banned full many a lake, and many a plain,
For trespass there committed! Let it be!
A Chief of souls he is! No signs we work,
Rulers earth-born: yet somewhat are we here -
Depart! By others answer we will send."

So Dairè sent to Patrick men of might,
Fierce men, the battle's nurslings. Thus they spake:
"High region for high heads! If build ye must,
Build on the plain: the hill is Dairè's right:
Church site he grants you, and the field around."
And Patrick, glancing from his Office Book,
Made answer, "Deo Gratias," and no more.

Upon that plain he built a little church
Ere long, a convent likewise, girt with mound
Banked from the meadow loam, and deftly set
With stone, and fence, and woody palisade,
That neither warring clans, far heard by day,
Might hurt his cloistered charge, nor wolves by night,
Howling in woods; and there he served the Lord.

But Dairè scorned the Saint, and grudged his gift,
Though small; and half in spleen, and half in greed,
Sent down two stately coursers all night long
To graze the deep sweet pasture round the church:
Ill deed: - and so, for guerdon of that sin,
Dead lay the coursers twain at the break of dawn.
Then fled the servants back, and told their lord,
Fearing for negligence rebuke and scath,

"Thy Christian slew the coursers!" and the king
Gave word to slay or bind him. But from God
A sickness fell on Dairè nigh to death
That day and night. When morning brake, the queen,
A woman leal with kind barbaric heart,
Her bosom from the sick man's head withdrew
A moment while he slept; and, round her gazing,
Closed with both hands upon a liegeman's arm,
And sped him to the Saint for pardon and peace.
Then Patrick, dipping in the inviolate fount
A chalice, blessed the water, with command
"Sprinkle the stately coursers and the king; "
And straightway as from death the king arose,
And rose from death the coursers.

Dairè then,
His tall frame boastful with that life renewed,
Took with him men, and down the stone-paved hill Rode
from his tower, and through the woodlands green, And
bare with him an offering of those days,
A brazen cauldron vast. Embossed it shone
With sculptured shapes. On one side hunters rode:
Low stretched their steeds: the dogs pulled down the stag
Unseen, except the branching horns that rose
Like hands in protest. Feasters, on the other,
Raised high the cup pledging the safe return.
This offering Dairè brought, and, entering, spake:
"A gift for guerdon and for grace, O Priest!"
And Patrick, upward glancing from his book,
Made answer, "Deo Gratias!" and no more.

King Dairè, homeward riding with knit brow
Muttered, "Churl's welcome for a kingly boon!"
And, drinking late that night the stormy breath
Of others' anger blent with his, commanded,
"Ride forth at morn and bring me back my gift!
Spurn it he shall not, though he prize it not."
They heard him, and obeyed. At noon the king Demanded
thus, "What answer made the Saint?"
They said, "His eyes he raised not from his book,

But answered, 'Deo Gratias!' and no more."

Then Dairè stamped his foot, like war-horse stung
By gadfly: musing next, and mute he sat
A space, and lastly roared great laughter peals
Till roared in mockery back the raftered roof,
And clashed his hands together shouting thus:
"A gift, and 'Deo Gratias!' - gift withdrawn,
And 'Deo Gratias!' Sooth, the word is good!
Madman is this, or man of God? We'll know!"
So from his frowning fortress once again
Adown the resonant road o'er street and bridge
Rode Dairè, at his right the queen in fear,
With dumbly pleading countenance; close behind,
With tangled locks and loose-hung battle-axe
Ran the wild kerne; and loud the bull-horn blew.
The convent reached, King Dairè from his horse
Flung his great limbs, and at the doorway towered
In gazing stern: the queen beside him stood,
Her lustrous violet eyes all lost in tears:
One hand on Dairè's garment lay like light
Wandering on dusky ripple; one, upraised,
Held in the high-necked horse that champed the bit,
His head near hers. Within, the man of God,
Sole-sitting, read his office book unmoved,
And ending fixed his keen eye on the king,
Not rising from his seat.

Then fell from God
Insight on Dairè, and aloud he cried,
"A kingly man, of mind unmovable
Art thou; and as the rock beneath my tower
Shakes not in storm so shakes not heart of thine:
Such men are of the height and not the plain:
Therefore that hill to thee I grant unsought
Which whilome I refused. Possession take
This day, lest hostile demon warp my mood;
And build thereon thy church. The same shall stand
Strong mother-church of all thy great clan Christ!"

Thus Dairè spake; and Patrick, at his word
Rising, gave thanks to God, and to the king
High blessing heard in heaven; and making sign
Went forth, attended by his priestly train,
Benignus first, his dearest, then the rest.
In circuit thrice they girt that hill, and sang
Anthem first heard when unto God was vowed
That House which David offered in his heart
His son in act, and hymn of holy Church
Hailing that city like a bride attired,
From heaven to earth descending. With them sang
An angel choir above them borne. The birds
Forbore their songs, listening that angel strain,
Ethereal music and by men unheard
Except the Elect. The king in reverence paced
Behind, his liegemen next, a mass confused
With saffron standard gay and spears upheld
Flashing through thickets green. These kept not line,
For Alp was still recounting battles old,
Aodh of wizards sang, and Ir of love;
While bald-pate Conan, sharpening from his eye
The sneering light, shot from his plastic mouth
Shrill taunt and biting gibe. The younger sort
Eyed the dense copse and launched full many a shaft
Through it at flying beast. From ledge to ledge
Clomb Angus, keen of sight, with hand o'er brow,
Forth gazing on some far blue ridge of war
With nostril wide outblown, and snorting cried,
"Would I were there!"

Meantime, the man of God
Had reached the fair crown of that sacred hill,
A circle girt with woodland branching low,
And roofed with heaven. Beyond its tonsure fringe,
Birch trees and oaks, there pushed a thorn milk-white,
And close beside it slept in shade a fawn
Whiter. The startled dam had left its side,
And through the dark stems fled like flying gleam.
Minded they were, the kernes, to kill that fawn,
And all the priests stood silent; but the Saint

Put forth his hand, and o'er her signed the Cross,
And, stooping, on his shoulder placed her firm,
And bade the brethren mark with stones her lair
Dewless and dusk: then, singing as he went
"Like as the hart desires the water brooks,"
He walked, that hill descending. Light from God
O'ershone his face. Meantime the awakened fawn
Now rolled her dark eye on the silver head
Close by, now turning licked the wrinkled hand,
Unfearing. Soon, with little whimpering sob,
The doe drew near and paced at Patrick's side.
At last they reached a little field low down
Beneath that hill: there Patrick laid the fawn.

King Dairè questioned Patrick of that deed,
Incensed; and scornful asked, "Shall mitred man
Play thus the shepherd and the forester?"
And Patrick answered, "Aged men, O king,
Forget their reasons oft. Benignus seek,
If haply God has shown him for what cause
I wrought this thing." Then Dairè turned him back
And faced Benignus; and with lifted hand,
Pure as a maid's, and dimpled like a child's,
Picturing his thoughts on air, the little monk
Thus glossed that deed. "Great mystery, king, is Love:
Poets its worthiness have sung in lays
Unread by ruder ones like me; and yet
Thus much the simplest and the rudest know,
Dear is the fawn to her that gave it birth,
And to the sceptred monarch dear the child
That mounts his knee. Nor here the marvel ends;
For, like yon star, the great Paternal Heart
Through all the unmeted, unimagined years,
While yet Creation uncreated hung,
A thought, a dawn-streak on the verge extreme
Of lonely Godhead's inner Universe,
Panted and pants with splendour of its love,
The Eternal Sire rejoicing in the Son
And Both in Him Who still from Both proceeds,
Bond of their love. Moreover, king, that Son

Who, Virgin-born, raised from the ruinous gulf
Our world, and made it footstool to God's throne,
The same is Love, and died for Love, and reigns:
Loveless, His Church were but a corse stone-cold;
Loveless, her creed were but a winter leaf
Network of barren thoughts, the cerement wan
Of Faith extinct. Therefore our Saint revered
The love and anguish of that mother doe,
And inly vowed that where her offspring couched
Christ's chiefest church should stand, from age to age
Confession plain 'mid raging of the clans
That God is Love; - His worship void and vain
Disjoined from Love that, rising to the heights
Even to the depths descends."

Conversing thus,
Macha they reached. Ere long where lay the fawn
Stood God's new altar; and, ere many years,
Far o'er the woodlands rose the church high-towered,
Preaching God's peace to still a troubled world.
The Saint who built it found not there his grave
Though wished for; him God buried otherwhere,
Fulfilling thus the counsels of His Will:
But old, and grey, when many a winter's frost
To spring had yielded, bent by wounds and woes
Upon that church's altar looked once more
King Dairè; at its font was joined to Christ;
And, midway 'twixt that altar and that font,
Rejoined his beauteous mate a later day.

THE ARRAIGNMENT OF SAINT PATRICK

Secknall, the poet, brings, in sport, three heavy charges against Saint Patrick, who, supposing them to be serious, defends himself against them. Lastly Secknall sings a hymn written in praise of a Saint. Saint Patrick commends it, affirming that for once Fame has dispensed her honours honestly. Upon this, Secknall recites the first stave, till then craftily reserved, which offers the whole homage of that hymn to Patrick, who, though the humblest of men, has thus arrogated to himself the saintly Crown. There is laughter among the brethren.

When Patrick now was old and nigh to death
Undimmed was still his eye; his tread was strong;
And there was ever laughter in his heart,
And music in his laughter. In a wood
Nigh to Ardmacha dwelt he with his monks;
And there, like birds that cannot stay their songs
Love-touched in Spring, or grateful for their nests,
They to the woodsmen preached of Christ, their King,
To swineherds, and to hinds that tended sheep,
Yea, and to pilgrim guests from distant clans;
His shepherd-worshipped birth when breath of kine
Went o'er the Infant; all His wondrous works
Or words from mount, or field, or anchored boat,
And Christendom upreared for weal of men
And Angel-wonder. Daily preached the monks
And daily built their convent. Wildly sweet
The season, prime of unripe spring, when March
Distils from cup half gelid yet some drops
Of finer relish than the hand of May
Pours from her full-brimmed beaker. Frost, though gone,
Had left its glad vibration on the air;
Laughed the blue heavens as though they ne'er had frowned,
Through leafless oak-boughs; limes of kindlier grace
And swifter to believe Spring's "tidings good"
Took the sweet lights upon a breast bud-swoll'n,
And crimson as the redbreast's; while, as when

Clear rings a flute-note through sea-murmurs harsh,
At intervals ran out a streak of green
Across the dim-hued forest.

From their wood
The strong arms of the monks had hewn them space
For all their convent needed; farmyard stored
With stacks that all the winter long had clutched
Their hoarded harvest sunshine; pasture green
Whitened with sheep; fair garden fenceless still
With household herbs new-sprouting: but, as oft
Some conquered race, forth sallying in its spleen
When serves the occasion, wins a province back,
Or flouts at least the foe, so here once more
Wild flowers, a clan unvanquished, raised their heads
'Mid sprouting wheat; and where from craggy height
Pushed the grey ledge, the woodland host recoiled
As though in Parthian flight; while many a bird,
Barbaric from the inviolate forest launched
Wild warbled scorn on all that life reclaimed,
Mute garth-still orchard. Child of distant hills,
A proud stream, swollen by midnight rains, down leaped
From rock to rock. It spurned the precinct now
With airy dews silvering the bramble green
And redd'ning more the beech-stock.

'Twas the hour
Of rest, and every monk was glad at heart,
For each had wrought with might. With hands upheld,
Mochta, the priest, had thundered against sin,
Wrath-roused, as when some prince too late returned
Stares at his sea-side village all in flames,
The slave-thronged ship escaped. The bishop, Erc,
Had reconciled old feuds by Brehon Law
Where Brehon Law was lawful. Boys wild-eyed
Had from Benignus learned the church's song,
Boys brightened now, yet tempered, by that age
Gracious to stripling as to maid, that brings
Valour to one and modesty to both
Where youth is loyal to the Virgin-born.

The giant meek, Mac Cairthen, on bent neck
Had carried beam on beam, while Criemther felled
The oaks, and from the anvil Laeban dashed
The sparks in showers. A little way removed,
Beneath a pine three vestals sat close-veiled:
A song these childless sang of Bethlehem's Child,
Low-toned, and worked their Altar-cloth, a Lamb
All white on golden blazon; near it bled
The bird that with her own blood feeds her young:
Red drops affused her holy breast. These three
Were daughters of three kings. The best and fairest,
King Dairè's daughter, Erenait by name,
Had loved Benignus in her Pagan years.
He knew it not: full sweet to her his voice
Chaunting in choir. One day through grief of love
The maiden lay as dead: Benignus shook
Dews from the font above her, and she woke
With heart emancipate that outsoared the lark
Lost in blue heavens. She loved the Spouse of Souls.
It was as though some child that, dreaming, wept
Its childish playthings lost, awaked by bells,
Bride-bells, had found herself a queen new wed
Unto her country's lord.

While monk with monk
Conversed, the son of Patrick's sister sat,
Secknall by name, beside the window sole
And marked where Patrick from his hill of prayer
Approached, descending slowly. At the sight
He, maker blithe of songs, and wild as hawk
Albeit a Saint, whose wont it was at times
Or shy, or strange, or shunning flattery's taint,
To attempt with mockery those whom most he loved,
Whispered a brother, "Speak to Patrick thus:
'When all men praised thee, Secknall made reply
"A blessed man were Patrick save for this,
Alms deeds he preaches not."'" The brother went:
Ere long among them entered Patrick, wroth,
Or, likelier, feigning wrath: - "What man is he
Who saith I preach not alms deeds?" Secknall rose:

"I said it, Father, and the charge is true."
Then Patrick answered, "Out of Charity
I preach not Charity. This people, won
To Christ, ere long will prove a race of Saints;
To give will be its passion, not to gain:
Its heart is generous; but its hand is slack
In all save war: herein there lurks a snare:
The priest will fatten, and the beggar feast:
But the lean land will yield nor chief nor prince
Hire of two horses yoked to chariot beam."
Then Secknall spake, "O Father, dead it lies
Mine earlier charge against thee. Hear my next,
Since in our Order's equal Brotherhood
Censure uncensured is the right of all.
You press to the earth your converts! gold you spurn;
Yet bind upon them heavier load than when
Conqueror his captive tasks. Have shepherds three
Bowed them to Christ? 'Build up a church,' you cry;
So one must draw the sand, and one the stone
And one the lime. Honouring the seven great Gifts,
You raise in one small valley churches seven.
Who serveth you fares hard!" The Saint replied,
"Second as first! I came not to this land
To crave scant service, nor with shallow plough
Cleave I this glebe. The priest that soweth much
For here the land is fruitful, much shall reap:
Who soweth little nought but weeds shall bind
And poppies of oblivion." Secknall next:
"Yet man to man will whisper, and the face
Of all this people darken like a sea
When pipes the coming storm." He answered, "Son,
I know this people better. Fierce they are
In anger; neither flies their thought direct;
For some, though true to Nature, lie to men,
And others, true to men, are false to God:
Yet as the prince's is the poor man's heart;
Burthen for God sustained no burden is
To him; and those who most have given to Christ
Largeliest His fulness share."

Secknall replied,
"Low lies my second charge; a third remains,
Which, as a shaft from seasoned bow, not green,
Shall pierce the marl. With convents still you sow
The land: in other countries sparse and small
They swell to cities here. A hundred monks
On one late barren mountain dig and pray:
A hundred nuns gladden one woodland lawn,
Or sing in one small island. Well - 'tis well!
Yet, balance lost and measure, nought is well.
The Angelic Life more common will become
Than life of mortal men." The Saint replied,
"No shaft from homicidal yew-tree bow
Is thine, but winged of thistle-down! Now hear!
Measure is good; but measure's law with scale
Changeth; nor doth the part reflect the whole.
Each nation hath its gift, and each to all
Not equal ministers. If all were eye,
Where then were ear? If all were ear or hand,
Where then were eye? The nation is the part;
The Church the whole" - But Criemther where he stood,
Old warrior, shouted like a chief war-waked,
"This land is Eire! No nation lives like her!
A part! Who portions Eire?" The Saint, with smile
Resumed: "The whole that from the part receives,
Repaying still that part, till man's whole race
Grow to the fulness of Mankind redeemed.
What gift hath God in eminence given to Eire?
Singly, her race is feeble; strong when knit:
Nought knits them truly save a heavenly aim.
I knit them as an army unto God,
Give them God's War! Yon star is militant!
Its splendour 'gainst the dark must fight or die:
So wars that Faith I preach against the world;
And nations fitted least for this world's gain
Can speed Faith's triumph best. Three hundred years,
Well used, should make of Eire a northern Rome.
Criemther! her destiny is this, or nought;
Secknall! the highest only can she reach;
Alone the Apostle's crown is hers: for this,

A Rule I give her, strong, yet strong in Love;
Monastic households build I far and wide;
Monastic clans I plant among her clans,
With abbots for their chiefs. The same shall live,
Long as God's love o'errules them."

Secknall then
Knelt, reverent; yet his eye had in it mirth,
And round the full bloom of the red rich mouth,
No whit ascetic, ran a dim half smile.
"Father, my charges three have futile fallen,
And thrice, like some great warrior of the bards,
Your conquering wheels above me you have driven.
Brought low, I make confession. Once, in woods
Wandering, we heard a sound, now loud, now low,
As he that treads the sand-hills hears the sea
High murmuring while he climbs the seaward slope,
Low, as he drops to landward. 'Twas a throng
Awed, yet tumultuous, wild-eyed, wondering, fierce,
That, standing round a harper, stave on stave
Acclaimed as each had ending. 'War, still war!'
Thou saidst; 'the bards but sing of War and Death!
Ah! if they sang that Death which conquered Death,
Then, like a tide, this people, music-drawn,
Would mount the shores of Christ! Bards love not us,
Prescient that power, that power wielded elsewhere
By priest, but here by them, shall pass to us:
Yet we love them for good one day their gift.'
Then didst thou turn on me an eye of might
Such as on Malach, when thou had'st him raise
By miracle of prayer that babe boar-slain,
And said'st, 'Go, fell thy pine, and frame thy harp,
And in the hearing of this people sing
Some Saint, the friend of Christ.' Too long the attempt
Shame-faced, I shunned; at last, like him of old,
That better brother who refused, yet went,
I made my hymn. 'Tis called 'A Child of Life.'"
Then Patrick, "Welcome is the praise of Saints:
Sing thou thy hymn."

From kneeling Secknall rose
And stood, and singing, raised his hand as when
Her cymbal by the Red Sea Miriam raised
While silent stood God's hosts, and silent lay
Those host-entombing waters. Shook, like hers,
His slight form wavering 'mid the gusts of song.
He sang the Saint of God, create from nought
To work God's Will. As others gaze on earth,
Her vales, her plains, her green meads ocean-girt,
So gazed the Saint for ever upon God
Who girds all worlds - saw intermediate nought -
And on Him watched the sunshine and the storm,
And learned His Countenance, and from It alone,
Drew in upon his heart its day and night.
That contemplation was for him no dream:
It hurled him on his mission. As a sword
He lodged his soul within the Hand Divine
And wrought, keen-edged, God's counsel. Next to God
Next, and how near, he loved the souls of men:
Yea, men to him were Souls; the unspiritual herd
He saw as magic-bound, or chained to beast,
And groaned to free them. For their sakes, unfearing,
He faced the ravening waves, and iron rocks,
Hunger, and poniard's edge, and poisoned cup,
And faced the face of kings, and faced the host
Of demons raging for their realm o'erthrown.
This was the Man of Love. Self-love cast out,
The love made spiritual of a thousand hearts
Met in his single heart, and kindled there
A sun-like image of Love Divine. Within
That Spirit-shadowed heart was Christ conceived
Hourly through faith, hourly through Love was born;
Sole secret this of fruitfulness to Christ.
Who heard him heard with his a lordlier Voice,
Strong as that Voice which said, "Let there be light,"
And light o'erflowed their beings. He from each
His secret won; to each God's secret told:
He touched them, and they lived. In each, the flesh
Subdued to soul, the affections, vassals proud
By conscience ruled, and conscience lit by Christ,

The whole man stood, planet full-orbed of powers
In equipoise, Image restored of God.
A nation of such men his portion was;
That nation's Patriarch he. No wrangler loud;
No sophist; lesser victories knew he none:
No triumph his of sect, or camp, or court;
The Saint his great soul flung upon the world,
And took the people with him like a wind
Missioned from God that with it wafts in spring
Some wingèd race, a multitudinous night,
Into new sun-bright climes.

As Secknall sang,
Nearer the Brethren drew. On Patrick's right
Benignus stood; old Mochta on his left,
Slow-eyed, with solemn smile and sweet; next Erc,
Whose ever-listening countenance that hour
Beyond its wont was listening; Criemther near
The workman Saint, his many-wounded hands
Together clasped: forward each mighty arm
On shoulders propped of Essa and of Bite,
Leaned the meek giant Cairthen: twelve in all
Clustering they stood and in them was one soul.
When Secknall ceased, in silence still they hung
Each upon each, glad-hearted since the meed
Of all their toils shone out before them plain,
Gold gates of heaven - a nation entering in.
A light was on their faces, and without
Spread a great light, for sunset now had fallen
A Pentecostal fire upon the woods,
Or else a rain of angels streamed o'er earth.
In marvel gazed the twelve: yea, clans far off
Stared from their hills, deeming the site aflame.
That glory passed away, discourse arose
On Secknall's hymn. Its radiance from his face
Had, like the sunset's, vanished as he spake.
"Father, what sayst thou?" Patrick made reply,
"My son, the hymn is good; for Truth is gold;
And Fame, obsequious often to base heads,
For once is loyal, and its crown hath laid

Where honour's debt was due." Then Secknall raised
In triumph both his hands, and chaunted loud
That hymn's first stave, earlier through craft withheld,
Stave that to Patrick's name, and his alone,
Offered that hymn's whole incense! Ceasing, he stood
Low-bowed, with hands upon his bosom crossed.
Great laughter from the brethren came, their Chief
Thus trapped, though late - he meekest man of men -
To claim the saintly crown. First young, then old,
Later the old, and sore against their will,
That laughter raised. Last from the giant chest
Of Cairthen forth it rolled its solemn bass,
Like sea-sound swallowing lighter sounds hard by.
But Patrick laughed not: o'er his face there passed
Shade lost in light; and thus he spake, "O friends
That which I have to do I know in part:
God grant I work my work. That which I am
He knows Who made me. Saints He hath, good store:
Their names are written in His Book of Life;
Kneel down, my sons, and pray that if thus long
I seem to stand, I fall not at the end."

Then in a circle kneeling prayed the twelve.
But when they rose, Secknall with serious brow
Advanced, and knelt, and kissed Saint Patrick's foot,
And said, "O Father, at thy hest that hymn
I made, long labouring, and thy crown it stands:
Thou, therefore, grant me gifts, for strong thy prayer."

And Patrick said, "The house wherein thy hymn
Is sung at morn or eve shall lack not bread:
And if men sing it in a house new-built,
Where none hath dwelt, nor bridegroom yet, nor bride,
Nor hath the cry of babe been heard therein,
Upon that house the watching of the Saints
Of Eire, and Patrick's watching, shall be fixed
Even as the stars." And Secknall said, "What more?"

Then Patrick added, "They that night and morn
Down-lying and up-rising, sing that hymn,

They too that softly whisper it, nigh death,
If pure of heart, and liegeful unto Christ,
Shall see God's face; and, since the hymn is long,
Its grace shall rest for children and the poor
Full measure on the last three lines; and thou
Of this dear company shalt die the first,
And first of Eire's Apostles." Then his cheek
Secknall laid down once more on Patrick's foot,
And answered, "Deo Gratias."

Thus in mirth,
And solemn talk, and prayer, that brother band
In the golden age of Faith with great free heart
Gave thanks to God that blissful eventide,
A thousand and four hundred years and more
Gone by. But now clear rang the compline bell,
And two by two they wended towards their church
Across a space for cloister set apart,
Yet still with wood-flowers sweet, and scent beside
Of sod that evening turned. The night came on;
A dim ethereal twilight o'er the hills
Deepened to dewy gloom. Against the sky
Stood ridge and rock unmarked amid the day:
A few stars o'er them shone. As bower on bower
Let go the waning light, so bird on bird
Let go its song. Two songsters still remained,
Each feebler than a fountain soon to cease,
And claimed somewhile across the dusking dell
Rivals unseen in sleepy argument,
Each, the last word: - a pause; and then, once more,
An unexpected note: - a longer pause;
And then, past hope, one other note, the last.
A moment more the brethren stood in prayer:
The rising moon upon the church-roof new
Glimmered; and o'er it sang an angel choir,
"Venite Sancti." Entering, soon were said
The psalm, "He giveth sleep," and hymn, "Lætare;"
And in his solitary cell each monk
Lay down, rejoicing in the love of God.

The happy years went by. When Patrick now
And all his company were housed with God
That hymn, at morning sung, and noon, and eve,
Even as it lulled the waves of warring clans
So lulled with music lives of toil-worn men
And charmed their ebbing breath. One time it chanced
When in his convent Kevin with his monks
Had sung it thrice, the board prepared, a guest,
Foot-sore and hungered, murmured, "Wherefore thrice?"
And Kevin answered, "Speak not thus, my son,
For while we sang it, visible to all,
Saint Patrick was among us. At his right
Benignus stood, and, all around, the Twelve,
God's light upon their brows; while Secknall knelt
Demanding meed of song. Moreover, son,
This self-same day and hour, twelve months gone by,
Patrick, our Patriarch, died; and happy Feast
Is that he holds, by two short days alone
Severed from his of Hebrew Patriarchs last,
And Chief. The Holy House at Nazareth
He ruled benign, God's Warder with white hairs;
And still his feast, that silver star of March,
When snows afflict the hill and frost the moor,
With temperate beam gladdens the vernal Church -
All praise to God who draws that Twain so near."

THE STRIVING OF SAINT PATRICK ON MOUNT CRUACHAN

Saint Patrick, seeing that now Erin believes, desires that the whole land should stand fast in belief till Christ returns to judge the world. For this end he resolves to offer prayer on Mount Cruachan; but Victor, the Angel who has attended him in all his labours, restrains him from that prayer as being too great. Notwithstanding, the Saint prays three times on the mountain, and three times all the demons of Erin contend against him, and twice Victor, the Angel, rebukes his prayers. In the end Saint Patrick scatters the demons with ignominy, and God's Angel bids him know that his prayer hath conquered through constancy.

From realm to realm had Patrick trod the Isle;
And evermore God's work beneath his hand,
Since God had blessed that hand, ran out full-sphered,
And brighter than a new-created star.
The Island race, in feud of clan with clan
Barbaric, gracious else and high of heart,
Nor worshippers of self, nor dulled through sense,
Beholding, not alone his wondrous works;
But, wondrous more, the sweetness of his strength
And how he neither shrank from flood nor fire,
And how he couched him on the wintry rocks,
And how he sang great hymns to One who heard,
And how he cared for poor men and the sick,
And for the souls invisible of men,
To him made way - not simple hinds alone,
But chiefly wisest heads, for wisdom then
Prime wisdom saw in Faith; and, mixt with these,
Chieftains and sceptred kings. Nigh Tara, first,
Scorning the king's command, had Patrick lit
His Paschal fire, and heavenward as it soared,
The royal fire and all the Beltaine fires
Shamed by its beam had withered round the Isle
Like fires on little hearths whereon the sun

Looks in his greatness. Later, to that plain
Central 'mid Eire, "of Adoration" named,
Down-trampled for two thousand years and more
By erring feet of men, the Saint had sped
In Apostolic might, and kenned far off
Ill-pleased, the nation's idol lifting high
His head, and those twelve vassal gods around
All mailed in gold and shining as the sun,
A pomp impure. Ill-pleased the Saint had seen them,
And raised the Staff of Jesus with a ban:
Then he, that demon named of men Crom-dubh,
With all his vassal gods, into the earth
That knew her Maker, to their necks had sunk
While round the island rang three times the cry
Of fiends tormented.

Not for this as yet
Had Patrick perfected his strength: as yet
The depths he had not trodden; nor had God
Drawn forth His total forces in the man
Hidden long since and sealed. For this cause he,
Who still his own heart in triumphant hour
Suspected most, remembering Milchoe's fate,
With fear lest aught of human mar God's work,
And likewise from his handling of the Gael
Knowing not less their weakness than their strength,
Paused on his conquering way, and lonely sat
In cloud of thought. The great Lent Fast had come:
Its first three days went by; the fourth, he rose,
And meeting his disciples that drew nigh
Vouchsafed this greeting only: "Bide ye here
Till I return," and straightway set his face
Alone to that great hill "of eagles" named
Huge Cruachan, that o'er the western deep
Hung through sea-mist, with shadowing crag on crag,
High-ridged, and dateless forest long since dead.

That forest reached, the angel of the Lord
Beside him, as he entered, stood and spake:
"The gifts thy soul demands, demand them not;

For they are mighty and immeasurable,
And over great for granting." And the Saint:
"This mountain Cruachan I will not leave
Alive till all be granted, to the last."

Then knelt he on the shrouded mountain's base,
And was in prayer; and, wrestling with the Lord,
Demanded wondrous things immeasurable,
Not easy to be granted, for the land;
Nor brooked repulse; and when repulse there came,
Repulse that quells the weak and crowns the strong,
Forth from its gloom like lightning on him flashed
Intelligential gleam and insight winged
That plainlier showed him all his people's heart,
And all the wound thereof: and as in depth
Knowledge descended, so in height his prayer
Rose, and far spread; nor roused alone those Powers
Regioned with God; for as the strength of fire
When flames some palace pile, or city vast,
Wakens a tempest round it dragging in
Wild blast, and from the aggression mightier grows,
So wakened Patrick's prayer the demon race,
And drew their legions in upon his soul
From near and far. First came the Accursed encamped
On Connact's cloudy hills and watery moors;
Old Umbhall's Heads, Iorras, and Arran Isle,
And where Tyrawley clasps that sea-girt wood
Fochlut, whence earliest rang the Children's Cry,
To demons trump of doom. In stormy rack
They came, and hung above the invested Mount
Expectant. But, their mutterings heeding not,
When Patrick still in puissance rose of prayer,
O'er all their armies round the realm dispersed
There ran prescience of fate; and, north and south,
From all the mountain-girdled coasts - for still
Best site attracts worst Spirit - on they came,
From Aileach's shore and Uladh's hoary cliffs,
Which held the aeries of that eagle race
More late in Alba throned, "Lords of the Isles" -
High chiefs whose bards, in strong transmitted line,

Filled with the name of Fionn, and thine, Oiseen,
The blue glens of that never-vanquished land -
From those purpureal mountains that o'ergaze
Rock-bowered Loch Lene broidered with sanguine bead,
They came, and many a ridge o'er sea-lake stretched
That, autumn-robed in purple and in gold,
Pontific vestment, guard the memories still
Of monks who reared thereon their mystic cells,
Finian and Kieran, Fiacre, and Enda's self
Of hermits sire, and that sea-facing Saint
Brendan, who, in his wicker boat of skins
Before that Genoese a thousand years
Found a new world; and many more that now
Under wind-wasted Cross of Clonmacnoise
Await the day of Christ.

So rushed they on
From all sides, and, close met, in circling storm
Besieged the enclouded steep of Cruachan,
That scarce the difference knew 'twixt night and day
More than the sunless pole. Him sought they, him
Whom infinitely near they might approach,
Not touch, while firm his faith - their Foe that dragged,
Sole-kneeling on that wood-girt mountain's base,
With both hands forth their realm's foundation stone.
Thus ruin filled the mountain: day by day
The forest torment deepened; louder roared
The great aisles of the devastated woods;
Black cave replied to cave; and oaks, whole ranks,
Colossal growth of immemorial years,
Sown ere Milesius landed, or that race
He vanquished, or that earliest Scythian tribe,
Fell in long line, like deep-mined castle wall,
At either side God's warrior. Slowly died
At last, far echoed in remote ravines,
The thunder: then crept forth a little voice
That shrilly whispered to him thus in scorn:
"Two thousand years yon race hath walked in blood
Neck-deep; and shall it serve thy Lord of Peace?"
That whisper ceased. Again from all sides burst

Tenfold the storm; and as it waxed, the Saint
Waxed in strong heart; and, kneeling with stretched hands,
Made for himself a panoply of prayer,
And wound it round his bosom twice and thrice,
And made a sword of comminating psalm,
And smote at them that mocked him. Day by day,
Till now the second Sunday's vesper bell
Gladdened the little churches round the isle,
That conflict raged: then, maddening in their ire,
Sudden the Princedoms of the Dark, that rode
This way and that way through the tempest, brake
Their sceptres, and with one great cry it fell:
At once o'er all was silence: sunset lit
The world, that shone as though with face upturned
It gazed on heavens by angel faces thronged
And answered light with light. A single bird
Carolled; and from the forest skirt down fell,
Gem-like, the last drops of the exhausted storm.

Then bowed the Saint his forehead to the ground
Thanking his God; and there in sacred trance,
Which was not sleep, abode not hours alone
But silent nights and days; and, 'mid that trance,
God fed his heart with unseen Sacraments,
Immortal food. Awaking, Patrick felt
Yearnings for nearer commune with his God,
Though great its cost; and gat him on his feet,
And, mile by mile, ascended through the woods
Till stunted were its growths; and still he clomb
Printing with sandalled foot the dewy steep:
But when above the mountain rose the moon
Brightening each mist, while sank the prone morass
In double night, he came upon a stone
Tomb-shaped, that flecked that steep: a little stream
Dropped by it from the summits to the woods:
Thereon he knelt; and was once more in prayer.

Nor prayed unnoticed by that race abhorred.
No sooner had his knees the mountain touched
Than through their realm vibration went; and straight

His prayer detecting back they trooped in clouds
And o'er him closed, blotting with bat-like wing
And inky pall, the moon. Then thunder pealed
Once more, nor ceased from pealing. Over all
Night ruled, except when blue and forkèd flash
Revealed the on-circling waterspout or plunge
Of rain beneath the blown cloud's ravelled hem,
Or, huge on high, that lion-coloured steep
Which, like a lion, roared into the night
Answering the roaring from sea-caves far down.
Dire was the strife. That hour the Mountain old,
An anarch throned 'mid ruins flung himself
In madness forth on all his winds and floods,
An omnipresent wrath! For God reserved,
Too long the prey of demons he had been;
Possession foul and fell. Now nigh expelled
Those demons rent their victim freed. Aloft,
They burst the rocky barrier of the tarn
That downward dashed its countless cataracts,
Drowning far vales. On either side the Saint
A torrent rushed - mightiest of all these twain -
Peeling the softer substance from the hills
Their flesh, till glared, deep-trenched, the mountain's bones;
And as those torrents widened, rocks down rolled
Showering upon that unsubverted head
Sharp spray ice-cold. Before him closed the flood,
And closed behind, till all was raging flood,
All but that tomb-like stone whereon he knelt.

Unshaken there he knelt with hands outstretched,
God's Athlete! For a mighty prize he strove,
Nor slacked, nor any whit his forehead bowed:
Fixed was his eye and keen; the whole white face
Keen as that eye itself, though - shapeless yet -
The infernal horde to ear not eye addressed
Their battle. Back he drave them, rank on rank,
Routed, with psalm, and malison, and ban,
As from a sling flung forth. Revolt's blind spawn
He named them; one time Spirits, now linked with brute,
Yea, bestial more and baser: and as a ship

Mounts with the mounting of the wave, so he
O'er all the insurgent tempest of their wrath
Rising rode on triumphant. Days went by,
Then came a lull; and lo! a whisper shrill,
Once heard before, again its poison cold
Distilled: "Albeit to Christ this land should bow,
Some conqueror's foot one day would quell her Faith."
It ceased. Tenfold once more the storm burst forth:
Once more the ecstatic passion of his prayer
Met it, and, breasting, overbore, until
Sudden the Princedoms of the dark that rode
This way and that way through the whirlwind, dashed
Their vanquished crowns of darkness to the ground
With one long cry. Then silence came; and lo!
The white dawn of the fourth fair Day of God
O'erflowed the world. Slowly the Saint upraised
His wearied eyes. Upon the mountain lawns
Lay happy lights; and birds sang; and a stream
That any five-years' child might overleap,
Beside him lapsed crystalline between banks
With violets all empurpled, and smooth marge
Green as that spray which earliest sucks the spring.
Then Patrick raised to God his orison

On that fair mount, and planted in the grass
His crozier staff, and slept; and in his sleep
God fed his heart with unseen Sacraments,
Manna of might divine. Three days he slept;
The fourth he woke. Upon his heart there rushed
Yearning for closer converse with his God
Though great its cost; and on his feet he gat,
And high, and higher yet, that mountain scaled,
And reached at noon the summit. Far below
Basking the island lay, through rainbow shower
Gleaming in part, with shadowy moor, and ridge
Blue in the distance looming. Westward stretched
A galaxy of isles, and, these beyond,
Infinite sea with sacred light ablaze,
And high o'erhead there hung a cloudless heaven.

Upon that summit kneeling, face to sea
The Saint, with hands held forth and thanks returned,
Claimed as his stately heritage that realm
From north to south: but instant as his lip
Printed with earliest pulse of Christian prayer
That clear aërial clime Pagan till then;
The Host Accursed, sagacious of his act,
Rushed back from all the isle and round him met
With anger seven times heated, since their hour,
And this they knew, was come. Nor thunder din
And challenge through the ear alone, sufficed
That hour their rage malign that, craving sore
Material bulk to rend his bulk - their foe's -
Through fleshly strength of that their murder-lust
Flamed forth in fleshly form phantoms night-black
Though bodiless yet to bodied mass as nigh
As Spirits can reach. More thick than vultures winged
To fields with carnage piled, the Accursèd thronged
Making thick night which neither earth nor sky
Could pierce, from sense expunged. In phalanx now,
Anon in breaking legion, or in globe,
With clang of iron pinion on they rushed
And spectral dart high-held. Nor quailed the Saint,
Contending for his people on that Mount,
Nor spared God's foes; for as old minster towers
Besieged by midnight storm send forth reply
In storm outrolled of bells, so sent he forth
Defiance from fierce lip, vindictive chaunt,
And blight and ban, and maledictive rite
Potent on face of Spirits impure to raise
These plague-spots three, Defeat, Madness, Despair;
Nor stinted flail of taunt - "When first my bark
Threatened your coasts, as now upon the hills
Hung ye in cloud; as now, I raised this Cross;
Ye fled before it and again shall fly!"
So hurled he back their squadrons. Day by day
The hurricanes of war shook earth and heaven:
Till now, on Holy Saturday, that hour
Returned which maketh glad the Church of God
When over Christendom in widowed fanes

Two days by penance stripped, and dumb as though
Some Antichrist had trodd'n them down, once more
Swells forth amid the new-lit paschal lights
The "Gloria in Excelsis:" sudden then
That mighty conflict ceased, save one low voice
Twice heard before, now edged with bitterer scoff,
"That race thou lov'st, though fierce in wrath, is soft:
Plenty and peace will melt their Faith one day:"
Then with that whisper dying, died the night:
Then forth from darkness issued earth and sky:
Then fled the phantoms far o'er ocean's wave,
Thence to return not till the day of doom.

But he, their conqueror wept, upon that height
Standing; nor of his victory had he joy,
Nor of that jubilant isle restored to light,
Nor of that heaven relit; so worked that scoff
Winged from the abyss; and ever thus the man
With darkness communed and that poison cold:
"If Faith indeed should flood the land with peace,
And peace with gold, and gold eat out her heart
Once true, till Faith one day through Faith's reward
Or die, or live diseased, the shame of Faith,
Then blacker were this land and more accursed
Than lands that knew no Christ." And musing thus
The whole heart of the man was turned to tears,
A fount of bale and chalice brimmed with death -
For oft a thought chance-born more racks than truth
Proven and sure - and, weeping, still he wept
Till drenched was all his sad monastic cowl
As sea-weed on the dripping shelf storm-cast
Latest, and tremulous still.

As thus he wept
Sudden beside him on that summit broad,
Ran out a golden beam like sunset path
Gilding the sea: and, turning, by his side
Victor, God's angel, stood with lustrous brow
Fresh from that Face no man can see and live.
He, putting forth his hand, with living coal

Snatched from God's altar, made that dripping cowl
Dry as an Autumn sheaf. The angel spake:
"Rejoice, for they are fled that hate thy land,
And those are nigh that love it." Then the Saint
Upraised his head; and lo! in snowy sheen
Cresting high rock, and ridge, and airy peak,
Innumerable the Sons of God all round
Vested the invisible mountain with white light,
As when the foam-white birds of ocean throng
Sea-rock so close that none that rock may see.
In trance the Living Creatures stood, with wings
That pointing crossed upon their breasts; nor seemed
As new arrived but native to that site
Though veiled till now from mortal vision. Song
They sang to soothe the vexed heart of the Saint -
Love-song of Heaven: and slowly as it died
Their splendours waned; and through that vanishing light
Earth, sea, and heaven returned.

To Patrick then,
Thus Victor spake: "Depart from Cruachan,
Since God hath given thee wondrous gifts, immense,
And through thy prayer routed that rebel host."
And Patrick, "Till the last of all my prayers
Be granted, I depart not though I die: -
One said, 'Too fierce that race to bend to faith.'"
Then spake God's angel, mild of voice, and kind:
"Not all are fierce that fiercest seem, for oft
Fierceness is blindfold love, or love ajar.
Souls thou wouldst have: for every hair late wet
In this thy tearful cowl and habit drenched
God gives thee myriads seven of Souls redeemed
From sin and doom; and Souls, beside, as many
As o'er yon sea in legioned flight might hang
Far as thine eye can range. But get thee down
From Cruachan, for mighty is thy prayer."
And Patrick made reply: "Not great thy boon!
Watch have I kept, and wearied are mine eyes
And dim; nor see they far o'er yonder deep."
And Victor: "Have thou Souls from coast to coast

In cloud full-stretched; but, get thee down: this Mount
God's Altar is, and puissance adds to prayer."
And Patrick: "On this Mountain wept have I;
And therefore giftless will I not depart:
One said, 'Although that People should believe
Yet conqueror's heel one day would quell their Faith.'"
To whom the angel, mild of voice, and kind:
"Conquerors are they that subjugate the soul:
This also God concedes thee; conquering foe
Trampling this land, shall tread not out her Faith
Nor sap by fraud, so long as thou in heaven
Look'st on God's Face; nay, by that Faith subdued,
That foe shall serve and live. But get thee down
And worship in the vale." Then Patrick said,
"Live they that list! Full sorely wept have I,
Nor will I hence depart unsatisfied:
One said; 'Grown soft, that race their Faith will shame;'
Say therefore what the Lord thy God will grant,
Nor stint His hand; since never scanter grace
Fell yet on head of nation-taming man
Than thou to me hast portioned till this hour."

Then answer made the angel, soft of voice:
"Not all men stumble when a Nation falls;
There are that stand upright. God gives thee this:
They that are faithful to thy Faith, that walk
Thy way, and keep thy covenant with God,
And daily sing thy hymn, when comes the Judge
With Sign blood-red facing Jehosaphat,
And fear lays prone the many-mountained world,
The same shall 'scape the doom." And Patrick said,
"That hymn is long, and hard for simple folk,
And hard for children." And the angel thus:
"At least from 'Christum Illum' let them sing,
And keep thy Faith: when comes the Judge, the pains
Shall take not hold of such. Is that enough?"
And Patrick answered, "That is not enough."

Then Victor: "Likewise this thy God accords:
The Dreadful Coming and the Day of Doom

Thy land shall see not; for before that day
Seven years, a great wave arched from out the deep,
Ablution pure, shall sweep the isle and take
Her children to its peace. Is that enough?"
And Patrick answered, "That is not enough."
Then spake once more that courteous angel kind:
"What boon demand'st then?" And the Saint, "No less
Than this. Though every nation, ere that day
Recreant from creed and Christ, old troth forsworn,
Should flee the sacred scandal of the Cross
Through pride, as once the Apostles fled through fear,
This Nation of my love, a priestly house,
Beside that Cross shall stand, fate-firm, like him
That stood beside Christ's Mother." Straightway, as one
Who ends debate, the angel answered stern:
"That boon thou claimest is too great to grant:
Depart thou from this mountain, Cruachan,
In peace; and find that Nation which thou lov'st,
That like thy body is, and thou her head,
For foes are round her set in valley and plain,
And instant is the battle." Then the Saint:
"The battle for my People is not there,
With them, low down, but here upon this height
From them apart, with God. This Mount of God
Dowerless and bare I quit not till I die;
And dying, I will leave a Man Elect
To keep its keys, and pray my prayer, and name
Dying in turn, his heir, successive line,
Even till the Day of Doom."

Then heavenward sped
Victor, God's angel, and the Man of God
Turned to his offering; and all day he stood
Offering in heart that Offering Undefiled
Which Abel offered, and Melchisedek,
And Abraham, Patriarch of the faithful race,
In type, and which in fulness of the times
The Victim-Priest offered on Calvary,
And, bloodless, offers still in Heaven and Earth,
Whose impetration makes the whole Church one.

Thus offering stood the man till eve, and still
Offered; and as he offered, far in front
Along the aërial summit once again
Ran out that beam like fiery pillar prone
Or sea-path sunset-paved; and by his side
That angel stood. Then Patrick, turning not
His eyes in prayer upon the West close held
Demanded, "From the Maker of all worlds
What answer bring'st thou?" Victor made reply:
"Down knelt in Heaven the Angelic Orders Nine,
And all the Prophets and the Apostles knelt,
And all the Creatures of the hand of God
Visible, and invisible, down knelt,
While thou thy mighty Mass, though altarless,
Offeredst in spirit, and thine Offering joined;
And all God's Saints on earth, or roused from sleep
Or on the wayside pausing, knelt, the cause
Not knowing; likewise yearned the Souls to God
In that fire-clime benign that clears from sin;
And lo! the Lord thy God hath heard thy prayer,
Since fortitude in prayer - and this thou know'st," -
Smiling the Bright One spake, "is that which lays
Man's hand upon God's sceptre. That thou sought'st
Shall lack not consummation. Many a race
Shrivelling in sunshine of its prosperous years,
Shall cease from faith, and, shamed though shameless, sink
Back to its native clay; but over thine
God shall extend the shadow of His Hand,
And through the night of centuries teach to her
In woe that song which, when the nations wake,
Shall sound their glad deliverance: nor alone
This nation, from the blind dividual dust
Of instincts brute, thoughts driftless, warring wills
By thee evoked and shapen by thy hands
To God's fair image which confers alone
Manhood on nations, shall to God stand true;
But nations far in undiscovered seas,
Her stately progeny, while ages fleet
Shall wear the kingly ermine of her Faith,
Fleece uncorrupted of the Immaculate Lamb,

For ever: lands remote shall raise to God
Her fanes; and eagle-nurturing isles hold fast
Her hermit cells: thy nation shall not walk
Accordant with the Gentiles of this world,
But as a race elect sustain the Crown
Or bear the Cross: and when the end is come,
When in God's Mount the Twelve great Thrones are set,
And round it roll the Rivers Four of fire,
And in their circuit meet the Peoples Three
Of Heaven, and Earth, and Hell, fulfilled that day
Shall be the Saviour's word, what time He stretched
Thy crozier-staff forth from His glory-cloud
And sware to thee, 'When they that with Me walked
Sit with Me on their everlasting thrones
Judging the Twelve Tribes of Mine Israel,
Thy People thou shalt judge in righteousness.'
Thou therefore kneel, and bless thy Land of Eire."

Then Patrick knelt, and blessed the land, and said,
"Praise be to God who hears the sinner's prayer."

EPILOGUE. THE CONFESSION OF SAINT PATRICK

Before his death, Saint Patrick makes confession to his brethren concerning his life; of his love for that land which had been his House of Bondage; of his ceaseless prayer in youth: of his sojourn at Tours, where St. Martin had made abode, at Auxerres with St. Germanus, and at Lerins with the Contemplatives: of that mystic mountain where the Redeemer Himself lodged the Crozier Staff in his hand; of Pope Celestine who gave him his Mission; of his Visions; of his Labours. His last charge to the sons of Erin is that they should walk in Truth; that they should put from them the spirit of Revenge; and that they should hold fast to the Faith of Christ.

At Saul then, by the inland-spreading sea,
There where began my labour, comes the end:
I, blind and witless, willed it otherwise:
God willed it thus. When prescience came of death
I said, "My Resurrection place I choose" -
O fool, for ne'er since boyhood choice was mine
Save choice to subject will of mine to God -
"At great Ardmacha." Thitherward I turned;
But in my pathway, with forbidding hand,
Victor, God's angel stood. "Not so," he said,
"For in Ardmacha stands thy princedom fixed,
Age after age, thy teaching, and thy law,
But not thy grave. Return thou to that shore
Thy place of small beginnings, and thereon
Lessen in body and mind, and grow in spirit:
Then sing to God thy little hymn and die."

Yea, Lord, my mouth would praise Thee ere I die,
The Father, and the Son, and Holy Spirit
Who knittest in His Church the just to Christ:
Help me, my sons - mine orphans soon to be -
Help me to praise Him; ye that round me sit
On those grey rocks; ye that have faithful been,
Honouring, despite dishonour of my sins,

His servant: I would praise Him yet once more,
Though mine the stammerer's voice, or as a child's;
For it is written, "Stammerers shall speak plain
Sounding Thy Gospel." "They whom Christ hath sent
Are Christ's Epistle, borne to ends of earth,
Writ by His Spirit, and plain to souls elect:"
Lord, am not I of Thine Apostolate?

Yea, by abjection Thine, by suffering Thine!
Till I was humbled I was as a stone
In deep mire sunk. Then, stretched from heaven, Thy hand
Slid under me in might, and lifted me,
And fixed me in Thy Temple where Thou wouldst.
Wonder, ye great ones, wonder, ye the wise!
On me, the last and least, this charge was laid
This crown, that I in humbleness and truth
Should walk this nation's Servant till I die.

Therefore, a youth of sixteen years, or less,
With others of my land by pirates seized
I stood on Erin's shore. Our bonds were just;
Our God we had forsaken, and His Law,
And mocked His priests. Tending a stern man's swine
I trod those Dalaraida hills that face
Eastward to Alba. Six long years went by;
But - sent from God - Memory, and Faith, and Fear
Moved on my spirit as winds upon the sea,
And the Spirit of Prayer came down. Full many a day
Climbing the mountain tops, one hundred times
I flung upon the storm my cry to God.
Nor frost, nor rain might harm me, for His love
Burned in my heart. Through love I made my fast;
And in my fasts one night I heard this voice,
"Thou fastest well: soon shalt thou see thy Land."
Later, once more thus spake it: "Southward fly,
Thy ship awaits thee." Many a day I fled,
And found the black ship dropping down the tide,
And entered with those Gentiles by Thy grace
Vanquished, though first they spurned me, and was free.
It was Thy leading, Lord; the Hand was Thine!

For now when, perils past, I walked secure,
Kind greetings round me, and the Christian Rite,
There rose a clamorous yearning in my heart,
And memories of that land so far, so fair,
And lost in such a gloom. And through that gloom
The eyes of little children shone on me,
So ready to believe! Such children oft
Ran by me naked in and out the waves,
Or danced in circles upon Erin's shores,
Like creatures never fallen! Thought of such
Passed into thought of others. From my youth
Both men and women, maidens most, to me
As children seemed; and O the pity then
To mark how oft they wept, how seldom knew
Whence came the wound that galled them! As I walked,
Each wind that passed me whispered, "Lo, that race
Which trod thee down! Requite with good their ill!
Thou know'st their tongue; old man to thee, and youth,
For counsel came, and lambs would lick thy foot;
And now the whole land is a sheep astray
That bleats to God."

Alone one night I mused,
Burthened with thought of that vocation vast.
O'er-spent I sank asleep. In visions then,
Satan my soul plagued with temptation dire.
Methought, beneath a cliff I lay, and lo!
Thick-legioned demons o'er me dragged a rock,
That falling, seemed a mountain. Near, more near,
O'er me it blackened. Sudden from my heart
This thought leaped forth: "Elias! Him invoke!"
That name invoked, vanished the rock; and I,
On mountains stood watching the rising sun,
As stood Elias once on Carmel's crest,
Gazing on heaven unbarred, and that white cloud,
A thirsting land's salvation.

Might Divine!
Thou taught'st me thus my weakness; and I vowed
To seek Thy strength. I turned my face to Tours,

There where in years gone by Thy soldier-priest
Martin had ruled, my kinsman in the flesh.
Dead was the lion; but his lair was warm:
In it I laid me, and a conquering glow
Rushed up into my heart. I heard discourse
Of Martin still, his valour in the Lord,
His rugged warrior zeal, his passionate love
For Hilary, his vigils, and his fasts,
And all his pitiless warfare on the Powers
Of darkness; and one day, in secrecy,
With Ninian, missioned then to Alba's shore,
I peered into his branch-enwoven cell,
Half-way between the river and the rocks,
From Tours a mile and more.

So passed eight years
Till strengthened was my heart by discipline:
Then spake a priest, "Brother, thy will is good,
Yet rude thou art of learning as a beast;
Fare thee to great Germanus of Auxerres,
Who lightens half the West!" I heard, and went,
And to that Saint was subject fourteen years.
He from my mind removed the veil; "Lift up,"
He said, "thine eyes!" and like a mountain land
The Queenly Science stood before me plain,
From rocky buttress up to peak of snow:
The great Commandments first, Edicts, and Laws
That bastion up man's life: - then high o'er these
The forest huge of Doctrine, one, yet many,
Forth stretching in innumerable aisles,
At the end of each, the self-same glittering star: -
Lastly, the Life God-hidden. Day by day,
With him for guide, that first and second realm
I tracked, and learned to shun the abyss flower-veiled,
And scale heaven-threatening heights. This, too, he taught,
Himself long time a ruler and a prince,
The regimen of States from chaos won
To order, and to Christ. Prudence I learned,
And sageness in the government of men,
By me sore needed soon. O stately man,

In all things great, in action and in thought,
And plain as great! To Britain called, the Saint
Trod down that great Pelagian Blasphemy,
Chief portent of the age. But better far
He loved his cell. There sat he vigil-worn,
In cowl and dusky tunic hued like earth
Whence issued man and unto which returns;
I marvelled at his wrinkled brows, and hands
Still tracing, enter or depart who would,
From morn to night his parchments.

There, once more,
O God, Thine eye was on me, or my hand
Once more had missed the prize. Temptation now
Whispered in softness, "Wisdom's home is here:
Here bide untroubled." Almost I had fallen;
But, by my side, in visions of the night,
God's angel, Victor, stood as one that hastes,
On travel sped. Unnumbered missives lay
Clasped in his hands. One stretched he forth, inscribed
"The wail of Erin's Children." As I read
The cry of babes, from Erin's western coast
And Fochlut's forest, and the wintry sea,
Shrilled o'er me, clamouring, "Holy youth, return!
Walk then among us!" I could read no more.

Thenceforth rose up renewed mine old desire:
My kinsfolk mocked me. "What! past woes too scant!
Slave of four masters, and the best a churl!
Thy Gospel they will trample under foot,
And rend thee! Late to them Palladius preached:
They drave him as a leper from their shores."
I stood in agony of staggering mind
And warring wills. Then, lo! at dead of night
I heard a mystic voice, till then unheard,
I knew not if within me or close by
That swelled in passionate pleading; nor the words
Grasped I, so great they seemed and wonderful,
Till sank that tempest to a whisper: - "He
Who died for thee is He that in thee groans."

Then fell, methought, scales from mine inner eyes:
Then saw I - terrible that sight, yet sweet -
Within me saw a Man that in me prayed
With groans unutterable. That Man was girt
For mission far. My heart recalled that word,
"The Spirit helpeth our infirmities;
That which we lack we know not, but the Spirit
Himself for us doth intercession make
With groanings which may never be revealed."
That hour my vow was vowed; and he approved,
My master and my guide. "But go," he said,
"First to that island in the Tyrrhene Sea,
Where live the high Contemplatives to God:
There learn perfection; there that Inner Life
Win thou, God's strength amid the world's loud storm:
Nor fear lest God should frown on such delay,
For Heavenly Wisdom is compassionate:
Slowly before man's weakness moves it on;
Softly: so moved of old the Wise Men's Star,
Which curbed its lightning ardours and forbore
Honouring the pensive tread of hoary Eld,
Honouring the burthened slave, the camel line
Long-linked, with level head and foot that fell
As though in sleep, printing the silent sands."
Thus, smiling, spake Germanus, large in lore.

So in that island-Eden I sojourned,
Lerins, and saw where Vincent lived, and his,
Life fountained from on high. That life was Love;
For all their mighty knowledge food became
Of Love Divine, and took, by Love absorbed,
Shape from his flame-like body. Hard their beds;
Ceaseless their prayers. They tilled a sterile soil;
Beneath their hands it blossomed like the rose:
O'er thymy hollows blew the nectared airs;
Blue ocean flashed through olives. They had fled
From praise of men; yet cities far away
Rapt those meek saints to fill the bishop's throne.
I saw the light of God on faces calm
That blended with man's meditative might

Simplicity of childhood, and, with both
The sweetness of that flower-like sex which wears
Through love's Obedience twofold crowns of Love.
O blissful time! In that bright island bloomed
The third high region on the Hills of God,
Above the rock, above the wood, the cloud: -
There laughs the luminous air, there bursts anew
Spring bud in summer on suspended lawns;
There the bell tinkles while once more the lamb
Trips by the sun-fed runnel: there green vales
Lie lost in purple heavens.

Transfigured Life!
This was thy glory, that, without a sigh,
Who loved thee yet could leave thee! Thus it fell:
One morning I was on the sea, and lo!
An isle to Lerins near, but fairer yet,
Till then unseen! A grassy vale sea-lulled
Wound inward, breathing balm, with fruited trees,
And stream through lilies gliding. By a door
There stood a man in prime, and others sat
Not far, some grey; and one, a weed of years,
Lay like a withered wreath. An old man spake:
"See what thou seest, and scan the mystery well!
The man who stands so stately in his prime
Is of this company the eldest born.
The Saviour in His earthly sojourn, Risen,
Perchance, or ere His Passion, who can tell,
Stood up at this man's door; and this man rose,
And let Him in, and made for Him a feast;
And Jesus said, 'Tarry, till I return.'
Moreover, others are there on this isle,
Both men and maids, who saw the Son of Man,
And took Him in, and shine in endless youth;
But we, the rest, in course of nature fade,
For we believe, yet saw not God, nor touched."
Then spake I, "Here till death my home I make,
Where Jesus trod." And answered he in prime,
"Not so; the Master hath for thee thy task.
Parting, thus spake He: 'Here for Mine Elect

Abide thou. Bid him bear this crozier staff;
My blessing rests thereon: the same shall drive
The foes of God before him.'" Answer thus
I made, "That crozier staff I will not touch
Until I take it from that nail-pierced Hand."
From these I turned, and clomb a mountain high,
Hermon by name; and there - was this, my God,
In visions of the Lord, or in the flesh? -
I spake with Him, the Lord of Life, Who died;
He from the glory stretched the Hand nail-pierced,
And placed in mine that crozier staff, and said:
"Upon that day when they that with Me walked
Sit with Me on their everlasting Thrones,
Judging the Twelve Tribes of Mine Israel,
Thy People thou shalt judge in righteousness."

Forthwith to Rome I fled; there knelt I down
Above the bones of Peter and of Paul,
And saw the mitred embassies from far,
And saw Celestine with his head high held
As though it bore the Blessed Sacrament;
Chief Shepherd of the Saviour's flock on earth.
Tall was the man, and swift; white-haired; with eye
Starlike and voice a trumpet clear that pealed
God's Benediction o'er the city and globe;
Yea, and whene'er his palm he lifted, still
Blessing before it ran. Upon my head
He laid both hands, and "Win," he said, "to Christ
One realm the more!" Moreover, to my charge
Relics he gave, unnumbered, without price;
And when those relics lost had been, and found,
And at his feet I wept, he chided not;
But, smiling, said, "Thy glorious task fulfilled,
House them in thy new country's stateliest church
By cresset girt of ever-burning lamps,
And never-ceasing anthems."

Northward then
Returned I, missioned. Yet once more, but once,
That old temptation proved me. When they sat,

The Elders, making inquest of my life,
Sudden a certain brother rose, and spake,
"Shall this man be a Bishop, who hath sinned?"
My dearest friend was he. To him alone
One time had I divulged a sin by me
Through ignorance wrought when fifteen years of age;
And after thirty years, behold, once more,
That sin had found me out! He knew my mission:
When in mine absence slander sought my name,
Mine honour he had cleared. Yet now - yet now -
That hour the iron passed into my soul:
Yea, well nigh all was lost. I wept, "Not one,
No heart of man there is that knows my heart,
Or in its anguish shares."

Yet, O my God!
I blame him not: from Thee that penance came:
Not for man's love should Thine Apostle strive,
Thyself alone his great and sole reward.
Thou laid'st that hour a fiery hand of love
Upon a faithless heart; and it survived.

At dead of night a Vision gave me peace.
Slowly from out the breast of darkness shone
Strange characters, a writing unrevealed:
And slowly thence and infinitely sad,
A Voice: "Ill-pleased, this day have we beheld
The face of the Elect without a name."
It said not, "Thou hast grieved," but "We have grieved;"
With import plain, "O thou of little faith!
Am I not nearer to thee than thy friends?
Am I not inlier with thee than thyself?"
Then I remembered, "He that touches you
Doth touch the very apple of mine eye."
Serene I slept. At morn I rose and ran
Down to the shore, and found a boat, and sailed.

That hour true life's beginning was, O Lord,
Because the work Thou gav'st into my hands
Prospered between them. Yea, and from the work

The Power forth issued. Strength in me was none,
Nor insight, till the occasion: then Thy sword
Flamed in my grasp, and beams were in mine eyes
That showed the way before me, and nought else.
Thou mad'st me know Thy Will. As taper's light
Veers with a wind man feels not, o'er my heart
Hovered thenceforth some Pentecostal flame
That bent before that Will. Thy Truth, not mine,
Lightened this People's mind; Thy Love inflamed
Their hearts; Thy Hope upbore them as on wings.
Valiant that race, and simple, and to them
Not hard the godlike venture of belief:
Conscience was theirs: tortuous too oft in life
Their thoughts, when passionate most, then most were true,
Heart-true. With naked hand firmly they clasped
The naked Truth: in them Belief was Act.
A tribe from Thy far East they called themselves:
Their clans were Patriarch households, rude through war:
Old Pagan Rome had known them not; their Isle
Virgin to Christ had come. Oh how unlike
Her sons to those old Roman Senators,
Scorn of Germanus oft, who breathed the air
Fouled by dead Faiths successively blown out,
Or Grecian sophist with his world of words,
That, knowing all, knew nothing! Praise to Thee,
Lord of the night-time as the day, Who keep'st
Reserved in blind barbaric innocence,
Pure breed, when boastful lights corrupt the wise,
With healthier fruit to bless a later age.

I to that people all things made myself
For Christ's sake, building still that good they lacked
On good already theirs. In courts of kings
I stood: before mine eye their eye went down,
For Thou wert with me. Gentle with the meek,
I suffered not the proud to mock my face:
Thus by the anchors twain of Love and Fear,
Since Love, not perfected, gains strength from Fear,
I bound to thee This nation. Parables
I spake in; parables in act I wrought

Because the people's mind was in the sense.
At Imbher Dea they scoffed Thy word: I raised
Thy staff, and smote with barrenness that flood:
Then learned they that the world was Thine, not ruled
By Sun or Moon, their famed "God-Elements:"
Yea, like Thy Fig-tree cursed, that river banned
Witnessed Thy Love's stern pureness. From the grass
The little three-leaved herb, I stooped and plucked,
And preached the Trinity. Thy Staff I raised,
And bade - not ravening beast - but reptiles foul
Flee to the abyss like that blind herd of old;
Then spake I: "Be not babes, but understand:
Thus in your spirit lift the Cross of Christ:
Banish base lusts; so God shall with you walk
As once with man in Eden." With like aim
Convents I reared for holy maids, then sought
The marriage feast, and cried, "If God thus draws
Close to Himself those virgin hearts, and yet
Blesses the bridal troth, and infant's font,
How white a thing should be the Christian home!"
Marvelling, they learned what heritage their God
Possessed in them! how wide a realm, how fair.

Lord, save in one thing only, I was weak -
I loved this people with a mother's love,
For their sake sanctified my spirit to thee
In vigil, fast, and meditation long,
On mountain and on moor. Thus, Lord, I wrought,
Trusting that so Thy lineaments divine,
Deeplier upon my spirit graved, might pass
Thence on that hidden burthen which my heart
Still from its substance feeding, with great pangs
Strove to bring forth to Thee. O loyal race!
Me too they loved. They waited me all night
On lonely roads; and, as I preached, the day
To those high listeners seemed a little hour.
Have I not seen ten thousand brows at once
Flash in the broad light of some Truth new risen,
And felt like him, that Saint who cried, flame-girt,
"At last do I begin to be a Christian?"

Have I not seen old foes embrace? Seen him,
That white-haired man who dashed him on the ground,
Crying aloud, "My buried son, forgive!
Thy sire hath touched the hand that shed thy blood?"
Fierce chiefs knelt down in penance! Lord! how oft
Shook I their tear-drop sparkles from my gown!
'Twas the forgiveness taught them all the debt,
Great-hearted penitents! How many a youth
Contemned the praise of men! How many a maid -
O not in narrowness, but Love's sweet pride
And love-born shyness - jealous for a mate
Himself not jealous - spurned terrestrial love,
Glorying in heavenly Love's fair oneness! Race
High-dowered! God's Truth seemed some remembered thing
To them; God's Kingdom smiled, their native haunt
Prophesied then their daughters and their sons:
Each man before the face of each upraised
His hand on high, and said, "The Lord hath risen!"
Then, like a stream from ice released, forth fled
And wafted far the tidings, flung them wide,
Shouted them loud from rocky ridge o'er bands
Marching far down to war! The sower sowed
With happier hope; the reaper bending sang,
"Thus shall God's Angels reap the field of God
When we are ripe for heaven." Lovers new-wed
Drank of that water changed to wine, thenceforth
Breathing on earth heaven's sweetness. Unto such
More late, whate'er of brightness time or will
Infirm had dimmed, shone back from infant brows
By baptism lit. Each age its garland found:
Fair shone on trustful childhood faith divine:
Eld, once a weight of wrinkles now upsoared
In venerable lordship of white hairs,
Seer-like and sage. Healed was a nation's wound:
All men believed who willed not disbelief;
And sat in that oppugnancy steel-mailed:
They cried, "Before thy priests our bards shall bow,
And all our clans put on thy great Clan Christ!"
For your sake, O my brethren, and my sons
These things have I recorded. Something I wrought:

Strive ye in loftier labours; strive, and win:
Your victory shall be mine: my crown are ye.
My part is ended now. I lived for Truth:
I to this people gave that truth I knew;
My witnesses ye are I grudged it not:
Freely did I receive, freely I gave;
Baptising, or confirming, or ordaining,
I sold not things divine. Of mine own store
Ofttimes the hire of fifteen men I paid
For guard where bandits lurked. When prince or chief
Laid on God's altar ring, or torque, or gold,
I sent them back. Too fortunate, too beloved,
I said, "Can he Apostle be who bears
Such scanty marks of Christ's Apostolate,
Hunger, and thirst, and scorn of men?" For this,
Those pains they spared I spared not to myself,
The body's daily death. I make not boast:
What boast have I? If God His servant raised,
He knoweth - not ye - how oft I fell; how low;
How oft in faithless longings yearned my heart
For faces of His Saints in mine own land,
Remembered fields far off. This, too, He knoweth,
How perilous is the path of great attempts,
How oft pride meets us on the storm-vexed height,
Pride, or some sting its scourge. My hope is He:
His hand, my help so long, will loose me never:
And, thanks to God, the sheltering grave is near.

How still this eve! The morn was racked with storm:
'Tis past; the skylark sings; the tide at flood
Sighs a soft joy: alone those lines of weed
Report the wrath foregone. Yon watery plain
Far shines, a mingled sea of glass and fire,
Even as that Beatific Sea outspread
Before the Throne of God. 'Tis Paschal Tide; -
O sorrowful, O blissful Paschal Tide!
Fain would I die on Holy Saturday;
For then, as now, the storm is past - the woe;
And, somewhere 'mid the shades of Olivet
Lies sealed the sacred cave of that Repose

Watched by the Holy Women. Earth, that sing'st,
Since first He made thee, thy Creator's praise,
Sing, sing, thy Saviour's! Myriad-minded sea,
How that bright secret thrills thy rippling lips
Which shake, yet speak not! Thou that mad'st the worlds,
Man, too, Thou mad'st; within Thy Hands the life
Of each was shapen, and new-wov'n ran out,
New-willed each moment. What makes up that life?
Love infinite, and nothing else save love!
Help ere need came, deliverance ere defeat;
At every step an angel to sustain us,
An angel to retrieve! My years are gone:
Sweet were they with a sweetness felt but half
Till now; - not half discerned. Those blessèd years
I would re-live, deferring thus so long
The Vision of Thy Face, if thus with gaze
Cast backward I might *see* that guiding hand
Step after step, and kiss it.

Happy isle!
Be true; for God hath graved on thee His Name:
God, with a wondrous ring, hath wedded thee;
God on a throne divine hath 'stablished thee: -
Light of a darkling world! Lamp of the North!
My race, my realm, my great inheritance,
To lesser nations leave inferior crowns;
Speak ye the thing that is; be just, be kind;
Live ye God's Truth, and in its strength be free!

This day to Him, the Faithful and the True,
For Whom I toiled, my spirit I commend.
That which I am, He knoweth: I know not now:
But I shall know ere long. If I have loved Him
I seek but this for guerdon of my love
With holier love to love Him to the end:
If I have vanquished others to His love
Would God that this might be their meed and mine
In witness for His love to pour our blood
A glad stream forth, though vultures or wild beasts
Rent our unburied bones! Thou setting sun,

That sink'st to rise, that time shall come at last
When in thy splendours thou shalt rise no more;
And, darkening with the darkening of thy face,
Who worshipped thee with thee shall cease; but those
Who worshipped Christ shall shine with Christ abroad,
Eternal beam, and Sun of Righteousness,
In endless glory. For His sake alone
I, bondsman in this land, re-sought this land.
All ye who name my name in later times,
Say to this People, since vindictive rage
Tempts them too often, that their Patriarch gave
Pattern of pardon ere in words he preached
That God who pardons. Wrongs if they endure
In after years, with fire of pardoning love
Sin-slaying, bid them crown the head that erred:
For bread denied let them give Sacraments,
For darkness light, and for the House of Bondage
The glorious freedom of the sons of God:
This is my last Confession ere I die.

www.ingramcontent.com/pod-product-compliance
Lightning Source LLC
Chambersburg PA
CBHW051548010526
44118CB00022B/2619